DENNIS KNUTSON

T4-AEK-435

Accounting Classics Series

Editor

ROBERT R. STERLING

University of Kansas

Publication of this Classic was made possible
by a grant from Price Waterhouse Foundation

Suggestions of titles to be included
in the Series are solicited and should
be addressed to the Editor.

ACCOUNTING PUBLICATIONS OF SCHOLARS BOOK CO.

Sidney S. Alexander et al., *Five Monographs on Business Income*
F. Sewell Bray, *The Accounting Mission*
Henry Rand Hatfield, *Accounting: Its Principles and Problems*
Bishop Carlton Hunt (Editor), *George Oliver May: Twenty-Five Years of Accounting Responsibility*
Kenneth MacNeal, *Truth in Accounting*
George O. May, *Financial Accounting: A Distillation of Experience*
William A. Paton, *Accounting Theory*
William Z. Ripley, *Main Street and Wall Street*
DR Scott, *The Cultural Significance of Accounts*
Charles E. Sprague, *The Philosophy of Accounts*
George Staubus, *A Theory of Accounting to Investors*
Robert R. Sterling (Editor), *Asset Valuation and Income Determination: A Consideration of the Alternatives*
Robert R. Sterling (Editor), *Institutional Issues in Public Accounting*
Robert R. Sterling (Editor), *Research Methodology in Accounting*

THE CULTURAL SIGNIFICANCE
OF ACCOUNTS

by

DR SCOTT

Professor of Accounting and Statistics
University of Missouri

Scholars Book Co.
Box 3344
Lawrence, Kansas 66044

Reprinted 1973 by
Scholars Book Co.

Library of Congress Card Catalog Number: 73-84524
Manufactured in the United States of America

THIS BOOK IS DEDICATED TO THOSE WHOSE INFLUENCE HAS CONTRIBUTED MOST TO IT: TO PROF. F. W. TAUSSIG AND TO THE MEMORIES OF THE LATE PROFS. H. J. DAVENPORT AND THORSTEIN VEBLEN.

PREFACE

This preface is a personal note to the reader.

When I was a student in the University of Missouri there was presented there a series of non-technical lectures given by professors from the different scientific departments. In varying ways and phraseology, each speaker during the series presented his subject as occupying the center of the scientific stage and accorded each of the other sciences a decidedly subordinate rôle. Even the philosopher who closed the series was as guilty as the rest. In fact he appropriated the whole stage.

It appeared to me then that each professor was so prejudiced by work in his special field that he was unable to give an unbiased appraisal of his subject. Not until several years later did it occur to me that the more penetrating and fundamental the work in any science is, the more that science becomes a real center of all human experience. The fault in that series of lectures was, after all, only with the philosopher in his not making this truth clear at the time.

In the study and teaching of accounting, I have been impressed by the very great desirability of a statement of the significance of accounts in the larger field of economic relationships. In seeking to formulate such a statement I have been led to undertake an analysis of the economic organization of society from an accounting point of view. But since accounts are closely related also to other forms of social organization—notably legal and governmental organization—an analysis of economic organization alone has not been sufficient. It has been necessary to adopt an even broader point of view. The more I have thought about the problem, the larger it has become. The desired orientation of accounts has proved to be obtainable only through an interpretation of cultural organization which places accounts at the very center or pivotal point of that organization.

The present volume represents an attempt to carry out the above program. No effort at all has been made to introduce new materials into the dicussion. The materials presented are, in fact, quite conventional and sometimes even trite. Care has been taken to avoid giving any one of these conventional materials a strange or unusual interpretation. Nevertheless, the cumulative result sought is an unusual interpretation which presents them all in a new and different light. The intention throughout has been to advance the argument by new combinations of familiar materials much as we get a new effect by rearrangement of the furniture in a house.

It is customary to place acknowledgments in a preface. They serve a real purpose if they afford the reader some insight as to the fundamental background of the chapters to follow. Too often they betray a scrupulous anxiety to distribute equitably the hypothetical glory of publication.

In the present case I must acknowledge first my obligation to the late Prof. H. J. Davenport, whose death has occurred while I have been reading the proof of this volume. I am indebted to Professor Davenport for a

PREFACE

rigid training in the logical analysis of an economic organization around the market and for the personal inspiration which created my interest in the general field of economics.

To me Professor Davenport's work is essentially an appeal from the overabstractions of such economists as J. B. Clark and Alfred Marshall. It is an appeal to the hypothetical facts underlying his own system of individualistic entrepreneur economics. When the assumed facts of this system have not appeared to be representative of current economic affairs, a critical attitude instilled by Professor Davenport himself has left me skeptical of all economic analyses based upon the assumption of a competitive market.

To Prof. F. W. Taussig, I am indebted for an orientation in discussions of economic theory due largely to his sympathetic interpretation of the works of the English classical school.

To the late Prof. Thorstein Veblen, I am indebted for the viewpoint expressed in the following discussion.

Summarizing these obligations in a sentence, I am indebted to Davenport for skepticism, to Taussig for appreciation, and to Veblen for faith.

In a more immediate sense, I am very greatly indebted to the late Prof. Allyn A. Young under whose supervision work on this project was begun as a doctoral dissertation. His criticisms, given at different stages in its progress, aided greatly in the development of the argument. He disagreed with some of its essential features but he himself was the first to insist that agreement was not neces-

PREFACE

sary. As a matter of fact, a divergence of opinions tended to make his criticisms the more helpful.

To Professor Davenport, I am further indebted for his reading and criticising the manuscript in the course of its preparation.

DR Scott.

University of Missouri.

CONTENTS

CHAPTER		PAGE
	PREFACE	vii
I	INTRODUCTION	3
II	TWO FUNDAMENTAL ASSUMPTIONS	20
III	THE RISE OF MARKET CONTROL	34
IV	DISINTEGRATION OF MARKET CONTROL	62
V	THE DECADENCE OF VALUE THEORY	85
VI	THE BACKWARD OUTLOOK OF SOCIALISM	109
VII	THE SCIENTIFIC POINT OF VIEW	117
VIII	DEVELOPMENT OF MODERN BUSINESS MANAGEMENT	137
IX	THE PROCESS OF SOCIAL READJUSTMENT	157
X	SOME ASPECTS OF STANDARDIZATION	161
XI	NATURE OF LAW AND ITS RELATION TO THE MARKET	176
XII	THE MARKET AND ACCOUNTS	194
XIII	ACCOUNTS AND STATISTICS	208
XIV	GOVERNMENT, ACCOUNTS AND THE MARKET	225
XV	THE FUTURE OF ECONOMIC CONTROL	265
XVI	POSTSCRIPT	290
	APPENDIX A	307
	APPENDIX B	312
	INDEX	315

THE
CULTURAL SIGNIFICANCE
OF ACCOUNTS

CHAPTER I

INTRODUCTION

The purpose of this volume, as stated in the preface, is to present an orientation of accounts. The task undertaken is no less than an exposition of the place of accounts in the existing scheme of human affairs among peoples who make the largest use of accounting technique.

The current emphasis upon orientation in educational discussions is conclusive evidence that we do not now have a common standard or ideal of social organization by which to keep our bearings. If we had such an ideal we would be emphasizing it and adjusting our activities to it instead of expending so much energy upon indefinite efforts at orientation. Nevertheless, the attempt at orientation to things in general is at least an effort to bring some order out of a general chaos. A multitude of faltering trials will, in the usual course of events, finally result in a common conception or ideal of social organization.

In making an attempt to formulate an orientation for accounts, the writer does not undertake to relate them to a static standard or ideal. His purpose is rather to show their place in a process of social development. What is aimed at in the following chapters is the presentation of a series of snap-shots, as it were, upon which the reader is expected to exercise his imagination in constructing the outlines of an organized process of contemporary cultural evolution.

The fundamental basis of this suggested outline of cultural development is an assumption that cultural unity rests upon a viewpoint or a cultural philosophy characteristic of the group which is unified. This tacit assumption is a foundation underlying all of the more or less detached chapters. It will be described more fully in the next chapter which deals with fundamental assumptions.

PRELIMINARY STATEMENT OF CHAPTER CONTENTS

Following the discussion of fundamental assumptions in Chapter II, is a chapter devoted to "The Rise of Market Control." It presents economic organization around the market as a characteristic feature of a particular cultural system. It undertakes to show how the modern period in European history was initiated by the development of a distinct cultural scheme. This cultural scheme is presented as an historical example of social unity based upon a common or dominant philosophical viewpoint. The scheme is perhaps best designated as an individualistic system.

This historical interpretation of the development of the market is followed by two chapters dealing with current aspects of economic control by the market. The first of these chapters discusses factors tending to undermine the free market as an institution of economic adjustment. It is argued that a changed cultural situation has destroyed the fundamental foundations of the institution. The other chapter, entitled "The Decadence of

STATEMENT OF CHAPTER CONTENTS 5

Value Theory," is an argument that the new situation has undermined also the abstract theory of economic organization which was formulated during the ascendency of the market.

Following these chapters upon the market, is a brief criticism of socialism. Socialism claims to present a projection or prediction of development from the competitive economic régime. The purpose in bringing a consideration of the socialist movement into this discussion is to point out the fundamental error of its claim and to use that claim as a foil for the projection, or forecast, which is to be outlined in the later chapters of this discussion.

After the consideration of socialism, the argument turns to an appraisal of "The Scientific Movement." The scientific point of view is presented as a popular or mass viewpoint which is destined to shape the development of a new cultural scheme. This cultural scheme is cited as a prospective illustration of social unity based upon a common or cultural philosophy. The controlling influence of the scientific viewpoint is made the primary vehicle for prediction both as to cultural development in general and as to economic development in particular.

Chapter VIII, entitled "The Development of Modern Business Management," is primarily a description of how business enterprise is being changed by a new cultural situation. It shows how the viewpoint of management is being reshaped to fit a new dominant philosophy. Thus it presents the incidence of cultural change upon what has been the key factor of the competitive or individualistic economic régime.

Chapter IX is a mere parenthesis which need not be considered in this preliminary survey.

Chapter X, a discussion of "Some Aspects of Standardization," presents some of the more general effects of the cultural trend which is revolutionizing business management. It calls especial attention to the unequal extent to which the trend has affected organization for production and organization for the distribution of economic incomes.

Thus Chapters VII, VIII and X constitute a unit devoted to the appearance of a new cultural viewpoint and to some of its immediate effects.

In such a remoulding process as that by which a general cultural organization is reshaped to fit a new social philosophy, it obviously is necessary that there should be a powerful resistance to the change somewhere in the existing cultural structure. Otherwise society would become entirely fluid and nothing could save the group from disintegration. This necessary conservative resistance is afforded by law. Hence the inclusion, at this point in the discussion, of a chapter dealing with the rôle of law in the cultural development with which we are concerned. The chapter which serves this purpose is also linked into other parts of the discussion by specific treatment of relations of the law and the market.

Following the discussion of law, is a group of three chapters, viz., XII, XIII and XIV, dealing specifically with accounts. These chapters are devoted to discussion of the relations of accounts to the market, to statistics, to law and government and to economic organization in general. Taken together they constitute a discussion of the rise of accounting control. Although they are based upon historical materials, their essential characteristic is an effort to project a line of development into the future. A background for this effort is afforded by the earlier chapter upon "The Rise of Market Control."

The rise of the market and the rise of accounts offer material for an interesting comparison. The comparison, however, is not emphasized in this discussion. History does repeat itself or we could not undertake historical projection. But it repeats itself with significant variations. Instead of laying stress upon the parallel between market development and accounting development, the writer undertakes to emphasize the relation of accounting development to the new cultural viewpoint which is herein held to be reshaping the current institutional structure. This relationship is foundation for the historical projection, or prediction, which is attempted relative to economic control through accounts.

Chapter XV, on "The Future of Economic Control," is devoted to some general aspects of economic organization. It points out how our economic system as a whole already has passed out of the competitive régime. At the same time it indicates the nature of the process through which the details of economic organization are passing in the emergence of a new economic régime.

Obviously, such a discussion as is outlined above cannot run exclusively or even primarily in objective and quantitative terms. Nevertheless the writer takes as a controlling assumption the hypothesis that human actions, and therefore all social phenomena, are included in one mechanistic system with other phenomena. It will therefore be understood that when such terms as market control and accounting control are used, they are to be interpreted as signifying forms of mechanistic determination.

In the course of the discussion a place will be made for ideals of social organization. In fact the argument specifically predicts the appearance of a new scheme of social ideals in the relatively near future. But these ideals are assumed to be subordinate to the mechanistic hypothesis. They are admitted to the discussion as a necessary recognition of the fact that all of us do and will continue to think in subjective terms, at least as a supplement to objective analysis.

THE DEVELOPMENT OF THEORY

It is at this time a popular truism that the current vogue of statistical investigation in economics cannot produce significant results without being directed and controlled by abstract theory. Too frequently this truth is assumed to mean that such control of statistical investigation must be exercised by the prevailing neo-classical theory built up around the cost *vs.* utility system of value theory. It commonly is argued that the way of knowledge in economics is through a process of gradual revision and amendment of accepted doctrines. Such, for example, was the prevailing expression in a symposium on methodology at a round table meeting of the American Economic Association in December, 1927.[1]

Against this accretion theory of the advancement of economic knowledge it may be said that in its early form the currently accepted system of theory did not arise by accretions to a previous system of theory. It came about through the formulation of generalizations based upon observations in a concrete economic and social situation.

Abstractions, or generalizations, such as those which are set up in economics, political science and other branches of social science, are to be contrasted with the concrete phenomena of social affairs from which they are drawn. When a given system of abstractions comes to serve as an ideal of social organization it tends to promote changes towards conformity with that ideal and to resist changes away from it. Thus when an ideal is being established the emphasis of those who subscribe to it is upon the constructive value of changes towards conformity with it. But when an ideal of organization is effectively realized the emphasis of those who subscribe to it necessarily shifts to resistance to changes away from it. The persistent tendency to change, which is characteristic of social phenomena, arises in the concrete situation rather than in the abstractions or ideals which are drawn therefrom. If the facts did not insist upon changing, ideals once established as socially dominant would perpetuate themselves.

Since social changes do come, it becomes necessary to

[1] *Cf. American Economic Review (Supplement)*, March, 1928.

keep abstractions and ideals abreast of changes in the concrete social situation. It is not to be inferred that this statement contradicts the above assertion that the formulation of an abstract theory or ideal of social organization does influence social facts. The point to be made here is that when the prevailing system of theory and the existing order of facts part company, it is primarily the system of theory which must suffer readjustment in order to re-establish harmony between them. But whether this reformulation of abstractions can be accomplished most effectively by piecemeal revision or by a new general appeal to the concrete situation, is a question to be argued on its merits. An answer to the question is scarcely to be undertaken without reference to the nature of the process by which the concrete social situation changes. If the social organization of a given cultural group is assumed to develop through a single life cycle, the assumption bears directly upon the problem here raised. It lends support to the view that economic abstractions, among others, can best be kept up to date by a process of piecemeal revision. But if such a social organization passes through a succession of cycles or cultural periods in which the bases of organization are distinct, then it is reasonable to expect that new abstractions for each separate cycle will be obtained by a new general appeal to the concrete situation.

It may be repeated here that a fundamental premise adopted for the present discussion is the assumption that social organization or social unity rests upon the existence of a common philosophical outlook. This assumption is made the basis for interpretation of different periods of our cultural development. Thus this discussion runs upon the basis that there are distinct cycles or periods in the process of social change. And, therefore, it is held herein that a new appeal to the concrete situation becomes periodically necessary and inevitable. Of course it is assumed that the method of piecemeal revision of abstractions is inevitable between the times when the other method must be resorted to.

As the analysis herein to be presented indicates, two distinct dangers confront economic science at the present time. One of these dangers is that the influence of methods in older sciences may lead to an overemphasis upon narrow and detailed studies with too little attention paid to controlling generalizations. The other danger is that a recognition of the need for general hypotheses may lead to an acceptance of the assumptions underlying current economic theory as an adequate basis for the direction and control of detailed investigations. Either of these procedures is bound to be barren of significant results. As here argued, the real promise of advancement of economic knowledge lies in a combination of statistical investigation with new general hypotheses drawn from the current concrete situation just as the assumptions underlying currently accepted economic theory once were drawn from an earlier concrete situation.

In a discussion of "Economics as a Field of Research," the late Prof. Allyn A. Young advised students of economics to devote their efforts to an analysis of new materials, that is, to detailed investigations and to problems which have a narrow range.[2] The work of formulating new hypotheses and making new generalizations from old materials he reserved for the somewhat sporadic efforts of an occasional genius. He wrote as follows:—

"The man of genius may be able to see new sequences in the old materials that have been combed over by others, but the average investigator is surer of making his contribution if he gets hold of new materials, and uses them with the utmost care." (p. 20)

It is true that he would give free rein to investigators of proved ability. For example:—

"Let the individual investigator, therefore, if he has passed his apprenticeship and proved his quality, have all the encouragement, all the freedom, and all the assistance we can give." (p. 24)

Professor Young, of course, approved the use of statistical methods in economics. He recognized that such methods must be controlled by general hypotheses. But he would have students of economics put through an apprenticeship before giving them freedom to meddle with general theory. That is, they should learn to apply the statistical method and other methods under the direction and control afforded by currently accepted general theory. Of course the test of their apprenticeship under such conditions would be their ability to defend the general theory controlling their apprenticeship efforts. If a student so trained is unusually capable, he may be able to propose minor corrections of generalizations controlling his problem but that is as far as he can hope that his apprentice-

[2] *Q. J. E.*, Nov. 1927.

ship will lead. And after he has proved his ability at defending or correcting accepted doctrines in a small way, he is to be accepted into the freedom and full fellowship of the economics fraternity.

Unfortunately this view has been the prevailing one in the field. Is it any wonder that such apprentices go on defending the doctrines they were trained to defend? Is it any wonder that men with really new ideas are rare?

Professor Young deplored the rarity of new ideas and ascribed it to Providence, or chance, by crediting such ideas to genius. But apparently the fault really lies in the system of training applied to students of economics.

A division of labor in economics is both necessary and desirable. It is not, however, a division between work of genius and work of a routine sort carried on by ordinary human beings. The present situation requires much painstaking, detailed, quantitative investigation. It requires also the formulation of general hypotheses and general theory to control and direct such quantitative investigations. (And of course this fundamental control does not mean the immediate management of statistical research.)

These two types of requirements are so different that a process of specialization or division of labor is a necessary condition of effective cooperation. However, this does not mean that drill in one is a necessary preparation for the other. Neither does it mean that apprentices are expected to do the work of masters. What is required as a matter of apprenticeship is distinct preparation for each type of work. It is not to be expected that new general hypotheses and syntheses will be struck off by the hand of genius in perfected form. They are to be had by that same process of repeated trial and error which is characteristic of other aspects of scientific work.

The following chapters are offered as a contribution to the task of setting forth new hypotheses. They are offered without any proof or claim of genius on the part of the author and in the belief that none such is necessary. They represent an effort at cooperation in a task in which consciously cooperative effort has not been the rule. They are presented in the belief that the proposal of new hypotheses and the formulation of new generalizations drawn from a concrete situation afford the greatest present promise of advancement in economic science.

The foregoing argument may be summed up in a few direct propositions as follows:

1. The process of social change in which we live involves a series of cycles or distinct cultural periods.

2. Abstractions, or generalizations, such as a system of economic theory, tend to be conservative rather than revolutionary. Nevertheless, such abstractions must be kept abreast of cultural changes or they lose their validity.

3. Within the limits of a particular cultural cycle or cultural system, the method of piecemeal revision and amplification of abstractions is useful and valid.

4. But with a change from one cultural cycle to another it becomes necessary to set up new abstractions drawn directly from the new concrete situation rather

than from the old abstractions which were themselves drawn from an earlier concrete situation.

5. Men trained in the technique of making piecemeal revisions of theory are so nearly useless for purposes of a general revision that when they do accomplish anything looking in that direction it is ascribed to a mysterious quality called genius. Of course the use of the term genius here, as always, indicates merely that an explanation of the accomplishment to which it is applied lies beyond our present understanding.

6. The formulation of a new system of abstractions in economics, as in other social sciences, is to be achieved by a process of trial and error carried on cooperatively by a large number of individuals.

The last point in the above summary deserves further emphasis. It is to be remembered always that the classification of social phenomena into various divisions, like economics and political science, is a practical expedient hit upon to promote an understanding of human affairs. Such distinctions are clear cut as between the different perfected systems of abstractions, but when an appeal is made to the current concrete situation the distinctions tend to be obliterated. Hence when a general change in the cultural situation makes it necessary for the workers in each field to make a new general appeal to the *de facto* social organization, the reformulation of theory for each field is bound up with a rewriting of the relations and distinctions between the abstractions of that field and those of other fields. To give a single specific example, a reorganization of economics is closely and inextricably related to the rewriting of distinctions between economic organization and political or governmental organization.

Since the cultural change which necessitates new abstractions in one field of social study also makes them necessary in other fields, students of the different social sciences now find themselves working upon the same task, that is, a reinterpretation of current human society. Under these circumstances, the cooperative process of setting up new hypotheses and new assumptions necessarily over-reaches the boundaries of each social science and includes them all. This does not mean that all social scientists are to be expected to attack the problem as representatives of a single social science. Through allowing their efforts to supplement each other they may hope to arrive at redefinitions of their distinct points of view.

The following chapters are to be read with the idea in mind that they represent an effort to contribute to a cooperative undertaking which is as broad as the whole field of the social sciences. The writer believes that they contain fruitful ideas. The discussion in them runs to loose ends but it is the firm conviction of the writer that such ideas thus expressed are more valuable and more useful for purposes which are now important than they would be if they were imbedded in a closely articulated, clearly delimited economic argument.

It is not to be inferred that the notion of cooperation referred to in this chapter involves a formal joint action such as is represented by "cooperative research" in which men from different fields work together upon a single

THE DEVELOPMENT OF THEORY

project. Such undertakings constitute merely a symptom of the current status of the social sciences. The term cooperation is used here in the broader sense that the work of one individual may supplement that of others even though it is done independently. According to the view here presented constructive work in the field of general theory will be most effective if it recognizes specifically its cooperative character even though it is carried on independently. Such work is to be judged in relation to the constructive development of theory and not upon the basis of its own logical completeness or incompleteness.

The "cooperative research" project referred to above represents a somewhat mechanical method of attacking a real problem. It is here suggested that a much more important and more promising method is for independent workers to adopt a cooperative attitude.

The chapters of this discussion have been criticised as dealing with too many problems which are more or less loosely connected, "an annotation of the cosmos," as it were. But that particular characteristic is essential to their purpose. They are intended primarily to serve as a basis for further thinking on the part of advanced students whose ideas of economic and social phenomena are not already set in a particular mould.

One further point remains to be made in this connection in order to guard against misapprehension. While it is argued here that the time has come for rewriting economic theory, it does not follow that the old economic theory should be discarded forthwith. If the motor car you drive is three years old, it is quite out of date, but good economy does not necessarily require that it be scrapped now. A new model may be based upon new principles which are destined to revolutionize motor car service but at the same time it may still be in an experimental stage. When everything is considered the current service of the old car may actually be the better. This, however, does not mean that work upon development of the new model should be abandoned.

Those who propose the immediate and complete abandonment of the old economic theory, of various sorts, are like the spoiled daughter of the family who would dispose of last year's car because it is not up to date. But those who refuse to recognize the importance of formulating the new theory are like the grandfather who not so many years ago preferred Old Dobbin to any new-fangled horseless carriage on the market.

Students of economics should master the old economic theory of the different schools both because of the remaining serviceability in some of it and because they obtain thereby an historical perspective. It will help give them a catholic attitude which is as desirable in economics as elsewhere. Such an attitude is to be achieved by clear thinking about economics, present and historical, and it should afford an unbiased appraisal of both the old and the new in theory.

It must be confessed that the discussion which follows does not exemplify the spirit of a catholic viewpoint. Its bias is perhaps justified as an antidote to our inherited over-emphasis upon generally accepted doctrines.

But more fundamentally, the use of a limited viewpoint is dictated by the problem which is undertaken. Since it is a particular cultural situation which is being interpreted, the use of a particular emphasis is necessitated by the same considerations which govern the division of all knowledge into different fields.

CHAPTER II

TWO FUNDAMENTAL ASSUMPTIONS

Any attempted appraisal of the cultural significance of a major social phenomenon involves almost the whole range of human affairs. It cannot fail to require excursions into territories staked out and claimed by different social sciences. The undertaking is, therefore, peculiarly hazardous. Anyone who attempts to coordinate materials drawn from such divergent sources thereby sets himself up as a target for the sure aim of those who are familiar with fields upon which he is merely a poacher. He cannot in any manner escape the charge of being superficial. In the present case the writer will not attempt to escape the charge. Instead he will plead intentional superficiality, as judged from other points of view, in order to be as fundamental as possible in an appraisal of the essential significance of accounts.

Such a discussion as is here proposed cannot run in terms of technical accounting concepts. The language used cannot be that which is peculiar to the accounting field. This follows from the fact that the discussion will deal with outside relationships of accounts rather than with accounting technique or particular accounting problems. But if the purpose aimed at is achieved the mere lack of technical terminology will not keep the resulting discussion from being accounting theory of a vital sort.

What is true for accounting is true also for other special

fields from which materials will be drawn. The accepted concepts and charted procedures of other fields are not more apt for the purpose here in hand than are the peculiar concepts and terminology of technical accounting theory.

The foregoing sounds very much like planning an expedition into foreign territories by deliberately ignoring the signposts and avenues of travel established by persons familiar with those lands. Such an excursion seems to invite disaster. As examples have too often proved, it is easy to wander aimlessly about in the homeland of a single social science, in spite of its local guideposts. And how much easier still it must necessarily be to lose oneself in a discussion ranging over the whole process of cultural development!

However, it is not here proposed to set out without any direction finders whatsoever. Our disregard of local guideposts is not foolhardiness but a rational safeguard against the risk of getting ourselves lost. What we need is a compass not a set of signposts. The compass which navigators use is not limited to any particular locality. It knows no nationality or regional control. So the instruments of navigation which we here select must be as broad in the scope of their operation as the seas which we expect to explore. We must have general direction finders, not local ones. The coordination of materials drawn from different scientific fields must rest upon common foundations underlying all those sciences. Therefore, the primary purpose of this chapter is to set out two general assumptions which are expected to give direction and co-

DENNIS KNUTSON

herence to the discussion in later chapters in spite of the heterogeneous character of the content of that discussion. One of these two assumptions is a philosophical point of view and the other is an assumption with respect to the role of philosophical viewpoints in the process of cultural development. These two assumptions are depended upon to preserve our bearings during the course of a distinctly exploratory discussion.

With respect to time, this discussion will cover a period of more than a thousand years. It will lead back eight hundred years or more into our cultural antecedents and at times the implications of a forward perspective will extend, as a rough guess, perhaps three or four hundred years.

THE OBJECTIVE AND SUBJECTIVE POINTS OF VIEW

Philosophical viewpoints arise out of human experience. To a layman the philosophy of a given school is nothing more than a way of thinking. The opportunity for different philosophies arises from the fact that the fragmentary and disjointed experience of the individual is such that it makes him think differently at different times. At one time he is impressed with the invariable sequences in which certain experiences come to him. He stubs his toe in the dark and is convinced that objects are real apart from his perception of them. Putting together this notion and the conviction of an invariable sequence of phenomena, he arrives at a philosophy which interprets his experience as having to do with an objective reality whose parts are bound together in invariable relations.

In short, he adopts the habit of explaining experience in objective terms.

But when the individual comes to his own conduct, as a believer in objective philosophy would say, the invariable sequence of relationships is no longer obvious. Indeed it is not discernible. The combination of causes back of each action is so complex, the mechanism through which those causes work themselves out is so highly developed, that, as a result, the untrained individual loses sight of the causal relationship altogether. Because he is the focal point of adjustment he makes the mistake of the fly on the axle of the chariot and concludes that he is a free agent independent of the relationship of cause and effect. The results of his actions are conceived by him to be ends set up by himself acting as a free agent. He sums up his active life in a hierarchy of ends and gives attention to the selection of means by which those ends are to be achieved. Thus there arises the habit of thinking in terms of ends and of the relationship of means to an end. This habit illustrates the philosophical viewpoint which is called subjective, as it would be interpreted by a realist or one who holds to the objective viewpoint.

The subjective and objective points of view are not to be reconciled with each other. As philosophers mainly agree, the relationship of cause and effect does not apply to ideas and purposes subjectively considered. And, on the other hand, there is in an objective, causal viewpoint no place for consideration of ends as such or for the relationship of means to an end.

In examining his assumptions the social scientist needs

to agree with himself with respect to his use of the objective and subjective points of view. Shall he assume that all human actions, that is all social phenomena, are subject to analysis in objective terms? Or shall he assume that in human conduct he encounters something which is so different from the subject matter of physical science that an interpretation in terms of objective relationships does not always apply to it? Failure to take a position on this issue is very likely to be serious. Any attempt to straddle the issue leaves us with results which are no better than the raw uninterpreted experience of actual life which at different times impels both subjective and objective ways of thinking.

Sometimes a distinction is drawn between "pure science" and "applied science." Too often the distinction is basis for a comparison by which the virtue of "pure science" is extolled. "Pure science" is described as a search for scientific truth without any ulterior motive. It is not biased or curbed by the interests of practical human affairs. Its noble unconcern for human ends sets its devotees apart from men engaged in more mundane pursuits.

In point of fact, however, the notion of such a fraternity of devotees of "pure science" is pure myth. The investigator who emphasizes the fact that he is "carrying on" regardless of whether the results which he hopes to obtain will ever be of practical value to the human race, does not take a similar attitude towards the combined efforts of all such investigators. Even those who would base scientific investigation upon idle curiosity are prone to betray a conviction that they belong to a class whose members are entitled to more dignity and more recognition than are the various "Weary Willies" of wealth and poverty. Even in the most objectively minded scientist's unremitting application of the objective viewpoint there is a latent subjective attitude. The scientist, no less than other men, is subject to the common fate which experience imposes upon men in leading them to think sometimes in objective terms and sometimes in subjective terms.[1]

But, while there is no valid distinction between "pure science" and science of another sort, there is a proper distinction to be drawn between clear thinking and confused thinking. Experience does actually lead to the development of different and independent philosophical viewpoints. It does not follow, however, that a careful attempt to explain human conduct, or social phenomena, should therefore rest upon a multiple basis compounded from the subjective and objective points of view. If those two viewpoints could be combined they would not be independent. Attempts to combine them inevitably lead to confusion. Notwithstanding the fact that there is an unstated subjective attitude involved in his efforts, the physical scientist does not mix that attitude with his working assumptions. At least when he does so he falls short of the accepted standards of the craft. Surely it behooves the social scientist to be equally careful of his philosophical foundations!

[1] *Cf.* Perry, *Approach to Philosophy*, Ch. V.

A RÔLE OF PHILOSOPHICAL VIEWPOINTS IN CULTURAL DEVELOPMENT

The evolutionary character of culture is obvious. Nevertheless, the social sciences have made slow progress in the use of an evolutionary viewpoint. They have been handicapped by the fact that each has been concerned with abstractions dealing with a different aspect of a unified cultural organization. They have, therefore, been fragmentary in character. Attempting to formulate the problems of a particular social science in evolutionary terms has been very much like asking a biologist to study one sex in a biological descent without giving any attention to the opposite sex; in fact without assuming the existence of another sex.

There is no satisfactory general theory of cultural development to which the problems of a particular social science can be related. It is the absence of such a theoretical analysis which has made necessary a second fundamental assumption which relates to the rôle of philosophical viewpoints in cultural development. This second major assumption can, perhaps, be set forth best as a development from the so-called theory of economic interpretation of history.

The theory of economic interpretation of history, or perhaps more properly *an* economic interpretation of history, asserts that the fundamental economic basis of any people's culture shapes the whole institutional superstructure of the society in question. Prevailing methods of economic production and distribution are declared to be the dominant and determining influence in cultural organization.[2]

In the first place, the theory implies a unity of culture. If a process of development or evolution is assumed, the theory becomes one relative to the technique of that process. It runs to the effect that methods of production and distribution are continually in process of development whereas the institutional superstructure of society tends to be conservative and to perpetuate itself. The result is conceived to be a continuous conflict between the two, or more accurately perhaps, a lack of harmonious adjustment between them. Periodically, the strain from lack of adjustment becomes so great that one or the other of two results must come to pass. Either the prevailing scheme of institutions is remoulded to fit its altered economic environment, or the particular culture in question disintegrates and is supplanted by another.

It is to be observed, however, that even when adjustment is effected the process never quite works itself out to a conclusion. When a general adjustment has been effected the economic environment, which necessitated and determined the adjustment, already has undergone further change. The statement of the late Professor Cunningham that feudalism was out of date before it became established, is thus held to be applicable to all social organization.[3]

[2] The Marxian emphasis is upon technology. The writer's view on this point is that technology is itself a cultural matter and not an outside cultural determinant. *Cf.* note on p. 169 below.

[3] *Growth of English Industry and Commerce*, Vol. I, p. 135.

Perhaps, then, the fairest statement of the theory of economic interpretation, as a theory of social evolution, would be that there are periods of friction alternating with periods of relative adjustment. The periods of adjustment are those when there is a relatively close harmony between the institutional superstructure of society and its fundamental economic setting. The periods of conflict, or transition, are those when there is a maximum of friction between the two.[4]

Historical examples in which changes of methods of economic production have influenced other social adjustments have led some students of economics to a conclusion as to a general economic determination of such other adjustments. Adherents of this view frequently have been led to assume positions which cannot be convincingly defended. Their most common error is the notion that forms of economic activity influence directly each institution and make it over to fit a new environment. Such a view surely is untenable.

HOW INSTITUTIONS ARE MADE OVER

Members of a given cultural group commonly think alike to a large degree. We are familiar with the unify-

[4] No effort has been made here to present the position of any particular individual. However, the presentation most nearly embodies what appears to the writer to be the general position of the late Prof. T. B. Veblen. *Cf.* also Achille Loria's interpretation of Karl Marx in his *Contemporary Social Problems,* Ch. V; translated by Garner. For various economic interpretations *cf.* P. Barth's *Philosophie der Geschichte als Sociologie* (Bk. II, Ch. 6, Third edition).

ing influence of an attack upon any group from the outside. The degree of obvious unity resulting from such pressure is merely the accentuation of group unity already present. This unity becomes obvious even in times of peace when we observe the attitude of members of a group towards a foreigner.

Cultural groups do not, of course, coincide with political organization. Minority cultural groups in fact constitute a troublesome political problem. Cultural unity is a somewhat tenuous and unsatisfying concept but nevertheless it is very real. Anglo-Saxon culture; North European *vs.* South European cultures, and Occidental *vs.* Oriental cultures are concepts whose meaning is not to be ignored even though they are not neatly expressed in political institutions.

In any cultural group, conduct contrary to the group's most fundamental traditions, its most sacred taboos, is most severely censured. A general tendency to conformity is undeniable even though a great variety of institutions makes up the organized cultural scheme. Cultural unity is a coherence running through a multiplicity of institutions. The solvent in which these institutions are fused and moulded into such unity as they possess is not a physical environment but a common way of thinking or a common philosophical viewpoint. Particular institutions are not to be explained without reference to this group point of view. Whenever there has been an essential unity of the institutions of a given people there will be found to have existed among them a common fundamental point of view. If a general reorganization of the prevailing scheme of institutions of a given people becomes necessary, it can take place only through a process of fusion or recrystallization under the influence of a general solvent which takes the shape of a new philosophical viewpoint. This means that an economic environment does not either directly shape each institution in the cultural scheme or directly mould the scheme of institutions as a whole. The immediate influence shaping development of any new cultural scheme is a dominant philosophy.[5]

Of course the changed circumstances of their physical environment may and frequently do affect institutions directly. Such changes of institutions are, for example, inevitable when a people changes from nomadic to a settled life or moves from a moist to a dry climate or moves from mountains to plains. Indeed such changes frequently eliminate particular institutions entirely. A certain amount of direct interpretation is therefore possible. But to attempt to explain a long evolution of particular institutions by such direct relations alone would be very crude indeed. And more crude still would it be to try to explain, on that basis, a general remoulding of a given cultural scheme. Attempts to use such a short cut method have led to some bizarre results under the

[5] The term philosophy as here used does not refer to a system of theory formulated by professional philosophers. It signifies rather a common or group point of view which may on occasion serve as the foundation for a superstructure of systematic philosophy.

name of economic interpretation. Those results at least serve to show the limitations of the method.[6]

In our own cultural history we can observe a changing system of forms and methods of economic production and distribution; a changing social structure of institutions, and a changing dominant philosophy which shows a relationship of agreement with each of the other two. Treating these as different parts of a unitary process of cultural evolution, the question may be argued whether any one of the three gives direction to the whole process. The frequent apparent chronological precedence of change in the economic factor does not conclusively prove its dominance any more than the fact that the prow of a ship passes a given point in its course before the rudder does, proves that the prow is the dominant part of the mechanism giving direction to the ship's movements. It is obvious that a philosophy which comes to be dominant must be an active factor for a long time before it would be recognized as dominant. It is quite conceivable that there should be advanced some theory concerning itself with the evolution of philosophical viewpoints which would be more far reaching and more illuminating of the process of cultural development than is the theory of economic interpretation. With our present limited knowledge of social evolution, it would be premature to assign

[6] Even such plausible discussions as those of Achille Loria leave the unbiased reader with a feeling that very much has been left out of the picture. Such direct interpretation always ignores too much.

paramount importance to any particular factor. Even the emphasis here placed upon a cultural philosophy does not preclude an appeal from it to some other influence.

However, we are not here attempting to set up a general theory of cultural history. We shall not undertake to argue at length the question whether the economic factor does actually dominate the process of cultural evolution. Evidence which is incidental to our special investigation will be presented without any attempt to formulate a definite appraisal of the rôle of economic influences in the process. The only thing which we shall insist upon in this connection is that the immediately controlling influence shaping the development of any given cultural scheme is a prevailing philosophy, a common or dominant philosophical viewpoint. We shall argue that in any study of the development of a new cultural period, the philosophical viewpoint then prevailing affords the surest basis for a forward-looking analysis and interpretation of the process. But we shall not undertake to show that such common viewpoints always arise from one particular cause or set of causes.

SUMMARY

The two fundamental assumptions which have been adopted to guide the development of the following argument are as follows:

1. It is desirable, at this time, that discussions of social phenomena should be conducted with as consistent an emphasis upon the objective point of view as is customary in the physical sciences. That is, present promise

for advancement in the social sciences lies in an application to social phenomena of the viewpoint or philosophy which underlies scientific work in the physical and biological sciences.

2. Cultural unity is dependent upon the organizing influence of a generally prevalent philosophical viewpoint. Hence such a viewpoint is the best available tool for explaining and interpreting the development of a new cultural period.

The second of these two propositions is expected to take on more definite meaning as the discussion proceeds. Reasons for the time qualification in the first also will appear later.

CHAPTER III

THE RISE OF MARKET CONTROL

Any study of social phenomena running in evolutionary terms requires a more or less arbitrary decision as to the point in the developing process at which a beginning is to be made. In the present discussion it appears to the writer desirable to begin with the development of a competitive economic organization. The relations of accounts to the market will call for extended discussion later. But those relations are such as to make it desirable to discuss first the development of market control over economic activities.

Market control has been closely associated in economic discussions with the term laissez faire. Much has been written upon the subject under that title. Too much perhaps! The discovery that a relatively free conflict of economic interests could work out to the welfare of an economic group undoubtedly has led many writers on the subject to be too optimistic over the fancied beneficence of such an unhindered conflict of interests. The cry for freedom from interference with economic activities has itself sometimes constituted a most potent interference.

And, on the other hand, reaction against the dogma of laissez faire sometimes has led to a studious presentation of obvious and superfluous argument to the effect that there never has been and never can be a thoroughgoing laissez faire organization of society.

MARKET NOW LESS SIGNIFICANT

We are not here interested in the theory or policy of laissez faire in its usual narrow sense. As such it has passed out of the realm of pertinent economic discussion. We are, however, interested in the economic organization of the period with which the doctrine is associated.

The term laissez faire never was a fortunate selection. It represented a reaction against an earlier period rather than constructive thought about a new one. It was out of date and might well have been discarded at the time of Adam Smith.

Positively expressed, the belief in a general policy of laissez faire is a belief that the open market is an efficient means of economic control. Therefore we can very properly speak of a laissez faire period of our economic history. It is the period characterized by the placing of a maximum of responsibility upon the market as a means of control. It is with some of the origins of this period that the present chapter is concerned.

MARKET NOW BECOMING LESS SIGNIFICANT

The foregoing paragraphs contain the suggestion that the market is, or is coming to be, a thing of the past. This implication is true only in a qualified sense. Control by the market is a thing of the past in the sense that the market is moving back from its dominant position in economic organization to a position of secondary rank. New machinery of economic control is establishing its dominance over the market so that we now look forward to a period in which markets themselves will be controlled and other machinery will occupy the front rank position in economic organization.

The qualification that the market has always been limited and circumscribed by such non-economic factors as custom and law need not be argued here. It has been presented so many times that it may be accepted without another repetition.[1] The point here intended is that other economic machinery is taking precedence over the market in the direct control of economic processes. However, the qualification should be stated again that further limitation of the market's rôle does not imply its elimination altogether. The market may be counted upon to continue as an active economic institution even after it ceases to be the focal point of economic organization.

Argument as to the market's declining significance will be developed at various points in the following chapters. It might be argued plausibly on the other side of the issue that the organization of society for market control has never been so complete as at present. And the writer believes such a contention to be true. But formal organization for market control does not constitute a stable foundation for the continuance of market control. It might be argued with similar plausibility that legal and political institutions are now more thoroughly grounded upon individual rights than ever before. But proof of such a proposition does not argue stability of current legal and political institutions or prove that this is a period of individualism. A shift of emphasis from the

[1] Cunningham—"The Relativity of Economic Doctrine"—*The Economic Journal*, Vol. II, p. 1.

competitive adjustment of individual legal interests may conceivably provide a new system of law and cut the whole foundation from under the current formal organization.

It will not be contended in this discussion that the formal machinery of market control has become less complete or less general. Rather it will be argued that the fundamental foundations of the system of market control are disintegrating.

THE THEORY OF MARKET CONTROL

The theory of market control in a society organized economically around the market is a model of simplicity. The market is a piece of machinery which automatically weighs the contribution which each competitive interest brings to it and just as automatically doles out the equivalent which is taken away. It adjusts conflicting economic interests, controls production and determines the allocation of economic incomes. Its efficient operation presupposes freedom of action on the part of those who have recourse to it and justification of its findings is not far to seek upon the basis of natural rights assumptions. If a man is master of himself it follows that he may direct his own efforts and become the rightful master of the products of those efforts; admittedly within certain legal limitations. But since a man cannot satisfy all of his own needs, in a society where there is specialization, it follows, as a corollary, that he is entitled to goods which he may acquire from other individuals who are free like himself by exchange of goods produced by him for goods produced by them. In the process of specialization, furthermore, some individuals do nothing but buy and sell. The product of their efforts is the gain which accrues to them thereby. The stamp of the market is the only basis upon which their gain rests. Therefore the stamp of the market comes to be the justification for all incomes received through the operation of the market mechanism. The stamp of the market comes to prove economic productivity. Hence the paramount importance of keeping the market really free.

These few simple propositions sum up the logic of an economic organization which was centuries in developing. The proof of their significance is the development of an actual market control in which they were applied.

PREREQUISITES OF MARKET CONTROL

The competitive organization of society is in some senses at an opposite pole from the feudal organization. Regulation by competition presupposes the free initiative of individuals seeking each his own economic gain. Trading for profit is the foundation of the system, whereas within the agricultural feudal régime of the Middle Ages trading for profit was looked upon as anti-social much as horse trading was viewed in earlier agricultural communities in the United States. Under the feudal regime property advantages and income depended upon the individual's social status. In a competitive system the basis of income and property comes to be economic productivity. The amount of individual freedom which is assumed and is necessary in the latter system would have been inconceivable to persons living under the feudal régime.

Before market regulation of economic affairs could become the general rule there must have been a general development of habits of thought and action in terms of independent individual interests. There must also have developed legal and political organization consonant with such an economic régime. This, of course, does not deny the obvious fact that economic, political and legal institutions have developed side by side.

It would not be profitable to enumerate here in detail the specific prerequisites of a system of competitive market control. Development of the monetary mechanism, improvements in production and transportation, development of laws governing trading and all the various technical furnishings of a competitive system developed gradually as parts of a general process of cultural reorganization.

ORIGINS OF INDIVIDUALISM

In a discussion of the development of a competitive economic organization, it is to be admitted to start with that the medieval itinerant merchant was a prototype of the "homo oeconomicus" of abstract competitive theory. However, in a régime of status he was accepted as an exception to the general rule. His freedom from feudal ties made him a forerunner of the modern period. But how did it come about that the exception became the general rule?

The fact that the trader's viewpoint was adopted by

the cultural group as a basis of social organization is not to be credited in any exclusive way to commerce or to the merchant class. That merchant class furnished the seed, so to speak, from which the new period developed. But growth of that seed depended upon fertile soil—a favorable environment. The chief point of argument here to be advanced is that such a favorable environment was afforded by a growth of handicraft industrialism.[2]

The Marxian overemphasis upon technology is not justified.[3] However, the dogmatic propaganda of Marx should not lead us to neglect the real importance of the cultural discipline which he so stressed.

The rise of handicraft marked the close of the feudal period. The rise of handicraft technique and the specialization in production which it signified was quite as epochal as the later introduction of the factory system of production. The development of handicraft industry was fully as striking in its social consequences as the growth of our current industrial system gives promise of being.

The rise of handicraft was contemporaneous with the rise of a town economy. Whatever theory is adopted with regard to the origin of the medieval town, handicraft industry was an important basis of its rise to prominence.[4] Cities there were, of course, which existed

[2] For emphasis of the influence of commerce and the merchant class *cf.* Pirenne, *Medieval Cities*, Chs. V and VI. However, Pirenne does not entirely ignore the importance of industry.

[3] *Cf.* "The Technological Interpretation of History," by A. H. Hansen, *Quarterly Journal of Economics*, Vol. 36, p. 72.

[4] Ashley, *Surveys Historic and Economic*, pp. 167-212.

throughout the semi-barbaric, agricultural period which in North and Central Europe followed the fall of the Roman Empire. But it is not those cities with which the passing of feudalism is to be associated. The agricultural dominance of the feudal period was supplanted by a rise of urban life based definitely upon growing commerce and a growing handicraft industry.

Towns, of course, may be supported by commerce alone and it is true that in any "new country" commerce precedes the manufacture of goods for trade. Trade in the surplus of agricultural products typically precedes trade in home-manufactured products. Feudal agricultural communities were no exception to this rule. The appearance of merchant guilds in northern Europe prior to craft guilds is in consonance with this fact and perhaps in consequence of it.[5] However, the prompt appearance of craft guilds and their growth to prominence are evidence of an early and increasing significance of handicraft production.

The importance of this handicraft production, which is indicated by the history of craft guilds, lies in the fact that it was one of the principal bases of a town economy which brought an end to the agricultural dominance of the feudal period.

The change of the social center of gravity from the agricultural feudal organization to a town economy was largely a matter of the development of the town. In any such social situation, the chief factor making for the dis-

[5] Gross, *Gild Merchant*, p. 114. *Cf.* also M. M. Knight, *Economic History of Europe*, Ch. VI.

integration of the old order is the development of a new one.[6] Undoubtedly there was a revolt of individuals from the restraints of the feudal régime. The prohibition of Charles IV (1356), forbidding towns to receive runaway serfs, is alone enough to establish that fact.[7] But mere reaction against the old order did not establish a new one. When the serf became a free townsman he did not automatically become an individualist or a free man in the eighteenth century sense of the term. The spirit of solidarity of the town was essentially medieval. Citizens of the town enjoyed a communal freedom rather than liberty of individual initiative. A free town meant that the town became free from feudal overlordship. Thereby the townsman became a citizen of a free town but not in any other sense a freer citizen of the town than when it was subject to feudal overlordship. The town economy was not made by individualism. Rather its development was one of the antecedents of individualism.[8]

The period of northwestern European culture in which handicraft production was the dominant form of industry extends from the rise of a town economy to the industrial revolution. As here used handicraft production refers to a technique of production rather than the organization of craftsmen into guilds. This period includes, towards its close, a remoulding of institutions which affords the

[6] These statements do not belie the significance of improving agricultural technique in connection with the growth of towns.

[7] This fact is supported also by the provision in some town charters that villeins unclaimed for a year remained free. Gross, *Gild Merchant*, p. 8.

[8] *Cf.* Pirenne, *op. cit.*, Ch. VII.

theory of economic interpretation what is perhaps its strongest historical support. A religious revolution occurred which placed religious responsibility upon the individual. A political upheaval turned government upside down and made the individual, in theory at least, the initial source of authority. Economic organization developed to the point of establishment of a system based upon the free action of individuals.

These tremendous social changes were accompanied by others of lesser importance. They were, of course, not independent of each other but were all parts of a general trend of social development. Their striking similarity forces search for a common explanation. This similarity consists in a common emphasis upon the individual. Their underlying viewpoint is the same. It is a subjective, individualistic philosophy.

The religious, political and economic changes here referred to were mass movements in the sense that they drew their strength largely from the common life and prevailing habits of thought of the peoples among whom they occurred. But what explains the bent of those prevailing habits of thought?

The philosophy of individualism appears to have arisen out of an economic environment rather than to have determined that environment. The handicraft town economy which was in some ways distinctly individualistic in its discipline preceded the development of individualism as a prevailing social philosophy. Much is made in this discussion of the conjunction of an increasing commercial activity and the rise of handicraft industrialism. These two factors contributed largely to the development of a cultural situation in which social organization came to be based upon the principle of a free play and competitive adjustment of individual interests. Both the rise of commerce and the rise of handicraft industrialism appear to have preceded the development of an individualistic philosophy. To all appearances this sequence occurred without opportunity for predetermination of the environment by the later developed philosophical point of view.

The individualistic discipline of handicraft economy has various aspects. In the first place, the character of the craft organization, with its apprentices, journeymen and master workmen, placed before each individual the possibility of a progression from apprenticeship to the position of a master workman. The work of each individual stood out as his own to commend or to condemn him. The measure of a man's success depended in a direct and obvious fashion upon his ability and effort. Such a discipline tended strongly to develop thrift, industry, self-reliance and other individualistic habits of thought and action.

However, the most subtle and probably the most significant influence of handicraft was its bearing as a technology upon those who applied it, working as they did individually with their own hands. This discipline continued even after the disorganization and disappearance of craft organizations. It schooled the workman in individualistic habits of thought and thus created an environment favorable to a spread of the trader's individualistic or contractual point of view.

The essential spirit of guild regulation was not in the least individualistic or liberal. Nevertheless, the volume of guild regulations, increasing as it did during the period of craft organization, is circumstantial evidence of an opposing pressure towards individualistic, independent action. Handicraft as a technology induced individualistic action while the craft organization officially opposed it.

When we look back at guild regulations from a later date, they appear in the light of conservative obstructions to the development of a freely competitive economic organization of society.[9] But in comparison with feudal society there was within the limits of those regulations a freedom of action which was epochal in its departure from the feudal status of the individual.[10] In point of fact, guild-controlled handicraft industry constituted what was for the time a peculiarly effective combination of freedom and restraint. The period of its dominance was, as one might say, a period of incubation in the movement towards a freely competitive society organized around the open market. The fact that individualism

[9] Gross, *Gild Merchant*, p. 50.

[10] It is not strange that the spirit of guild control should be found to be contrary to the fundamental discipline afforded by the technology which it administered. A somewhat similar contradiction is to be observed now in economic organization for production and economic organization for distribution. *Cf.* pp. 166 and 167 below.

as a social philosophy did not make its appearance until after the passing of guild control does not belie the importance of even the guild period in a development of individualism.[11]

THE RENAISSANCE

The period when individualism actually made its appearance as a definite cultural movement, is called the Renaissance. The anonymity of the Middle Ages gave way to an expression of personality and individuality in letters, art and philosophy as well as in more practical activities. The writer well remembers his secondary school introduction to the Renaissance as a sudden, belated bursting forth of flower and foliage after a severe winter.

Such elementary presentations usually include a rather indiscriminatory count of causes back of the "re-birth of culture." First, the crusades which made the medieval

---

[11] It has been argued that individualism is essentially a racial trait; that it is an inheritance from the Teutonic ancestors of those who have made so much of it. This argument apparently would condemn the descendants of those German tribesmen to a perpetual individualism. The most that could be made of the argument would be a racial receptivity. Perhaps, as some woods are grained to take a higher polish, some peoples may be predisposed to individualistic habits. Biologists or psychologists may perhaps be able to make something of the argument.

It should be emphasized here that the handicraft period is not coincident with guild control. Handicraft as a technology continued after the disappearance of craft guilds and did not come to an abrupt end even with the industrial revolution. It might well be argued that the discipline afforded by handicraft as a technology brought about the disintegration of the craft guilds.

THE RENAISSANCE

man more cosmopolitan by opening his eyes to the existence of other cultures and at the same time caused a revival of commerce. Second, the revival of classic learning. Third, the shifting of interest from the next world to this, the study of man and his environment, the beginnings of modern science. Fourth, the rise of a spirit of adventure fostered by geographic exploration; etc., etc.

The errors of such an account are largely in its superficiality and in its failure to discriminate between two contemporaneous movements. Usually the significance of the crusades is overemphasized because of their spectacular character. So far as their bearing upon the movement towards individualism is concerned, their supposed influence can be discounted at something near 100 per cent bank discount. They did not initiate the development of a town economy even though they did in many cases result in an increased freedom of towns from feudal overlordship. But in spite of such incidental effects they did not substantially affect the course of town development. Even their relation to the growth of commerce may well be as an effect rather than a cause.[12] It may be confidently asserted that the economic life and habits of thought of the mass of European peoples of immediately succeeding centuries were not materially shaped by them.

However, it cannot be stated with similar assurance that the outlook of a more educated minority was equally unaffected by the crusades. Without doubt the crusades did give some who appreciated the significance of other

[12] *Cf.* Taylor, *The Mediæval Mind*, Vol. I, p. 333.

cultures a more objective, cosmopolitan point of view. Doubtless contact with and respect for the Moslems of the East made it easier to borrow from them and from the Moors of Spain. The revival of classic culture surely was stimulated by closer contacts with the East. Changes of viewpoint, resulting from new contacts, the notion of a science of nature, a separation of intellectual from religious interests and scattering accomplishments towards the establishment of modern sciences constitute a somewhat tenuous movement which undoubtedly was stimulated by the crusades. But the crusades surely did not initiate it.

This latter group of tendencies represents a drift towards more objective and more impersonal habits of thought. Confusion of this group of tendencies with a more prevailing drift towards individualism would be poor interpretation of both. Nor can one be made a part or an offshoot of the other. Martin Luther drew support for his break with the established church, not from the humanistic movement within the church, but from the everyday life of the mass of people to whom he appealed.[18] His dogma of salvation by faith with individual religious rights and responsibilities appealed to his contemporaries as reasonable because it fitted in with

[18] The immediate political and economic aspects of the German reformation could not be ignored in any explanation of it. However, they do not constitute the complete account. In any such social change the leaders of conflicting groups must deal with masses of individuals; with the raw material of social organization. Successful social engineering is dependent upon an organization of social materials which is analogous to the civil engineers' organiza-

their unconsciously acquired habits of thought. The subjective, individualistic character of the movement initiated by him is indicated by its distrust of reason. The fact that a man like Erasmus shows humanistic influence, or perhaps exerted a strong humanistic influence, and at the same time shows strong individualistic tendencies, does not serve to combine the two movements. It is not unusual to find even men of great ability showing the bias of influences which are contradictory in character.

The Renaissance, like many other cultural periods, shows the working of conflicting influences. It is best interpreted by separating those influences. The tendency towards an attitude of cosmopolitanism, the influence of classic literatures, the separation of religious and intellectual interests and the beginning of the modern scientific point of view, we have lumped together as constituting in a somewhat loose fashion a single thought movement. Perhaps it would be better to call them merely straws pointing in the same direction. Their common characteristics are that they represented a relatively objective point of view and they affected a comparatively small and relatively cultured portion of the population. Circumstances, however, were overwhelmingly against a popular development of such a viewpoint.

tion of physical materials. And the discussion at this point deals with the raw material of the German reformation rather than the social engineering which it involved.

Of course in any thoroughgoing objective analysis, social engineering would become just as matter of fact as the raw materials with which it functions. *Cf.* note p. 184.

It is here contended that the rise of North European states to economic and political strength rested upon a combination of handicraft industrialism with commercial enterprise. It is argued that the influence of handicraft industrialism upon the mass of town-dwelling population created a fertile soil for the spread of individualistic ideas.

Thus a tendency towards individualism and a tendency towards an objective and cosmopolitan viewpoint came out of the disintegration of medieval society side by side. The tendency towards individualism was a mass movement and its momentum, figuratively speaking, caused it to completely overshadow the other viewpoint. It made individualistic philosophers, statesmen and religious teachers, and, paradoxically, individualistic scientists as well. The subjective, individualistic point of view shaped the development of a new cultural organization. Under its dominance a certain amount of confusion of the two viewpoints was inevitable. It is quite to be expected that in such a period attempts to analyze and explain social phenomena should run largely in terms of the dominant point of view. Perhaps it was desirable that they should. At least it was inevitable.

It is a well-known characteristic of the "social sciences" that they frequently cater to both the subjective and the objective points of view. That confusion is a heritage from a cultural period dominated by an individualistic, subjective philosophy. It is to be interpreted as a common inheritance rather than as the result of logical errors perpetrated by particular individuals. It is a heritage which has affected all social sciences and has delayed their development quite as much as has the complexity of the phenomena with which they are concerned.

MEDIEVAL VS. MODERN CULTURE

The division between medieval and modern cultural history is broken and indistinct. Modern economic development may be definitely said to take its rise in Italy where it rested upon the basis of European trade with the East. Commercial methods, including accounting technique, were developed in Italy and borrowed by North European peoples. But when trade with Asia shifted to the sea route around Africa, Italian economic leadership vanished.

Following the period of Italian supremacy, Spain, through exploration and colonization, acquired control over a lion's share of the western hemisphere and made her bid for political and economic power. She failed even more signally than Italy.

Why was it that these two countries with such great early advantages were so thoroughly eclipsed by other nations? The answer is that the fundamental weakness of both Italy and Spain was their lack of developed industrial life. The more northern nations which surpassed them were producers of goods. If Italy had been as firmly established as a producer of staple goods as she was in commerce her leadership would not so readily have succumbed with the discovery of a sea route to India.

It is not here proposed to argue at length the question of the relative significance of trade and production as a basis for political power and cultural development.[14] Looking at the question from the viewpoint of Italian experience it appears that modern economic development got its start in the field of commerce, growth of which gave impetus to production. However, it is difficult to appraise the beginnings of handicraft production and to weigh them against the rise of commerce. For present purposes it is not necessary to decide the issue. In any case the modern economic period can be dated from the rise of Italian cities to prominence as centers of economic activity. Since that time there has been, in general, one continuous process of economic development with respect to both production and trade in North European and, latterly, in American countries.

When we turn to cultural organization the history of the Italian period does not so clearly connect with the later development in more northern countries. In culture as well as economic development Italy took the lead. Obviously the Italian Renaissance was a reaction against medievalism but there was a wide difference between it and the later movement in more northern countries. The Italian Renaissance was more of a resurrection of old culture than a rebirth. It was essentially pagan in its outlook. From an ethical point of view, it was distinctly lacking in moral stamina. The history of the period discloses a breakdown of old restraints without the development of new moral fiber.

[14] *Cf.* A. A. Young, Introduction to M. M. Knight's *Economic History of Europe*. In the writer's opinion Professor Young placed too exclusive an emphasis upon commerce or business.

The later developed Renaissance in protestant countries borrowed heavily from the Italian movement but it borrowed superficially. Its essential character was its own. In its viewpoint this protestant cultural revival was essentially Christian rather than pagan. It also displayed a vigorous ethical tone which was due, not to its religious coloring, but to a fundamental philosophical viewpoint underlying at the same time its religious, political, economic and other social developments. The protestant reformation was part of a general cultural reorganization.[15] And the soil in which the new cultural viewpoint developed was the discipline afforded by the conjunction of growing commerce with that same handicraft industrialism which served as a basis for the establishment of North European economic and political leadership.

Speaking roughly, the Italian Renaissance is to be associated with the thought movement towards a more impersonal and objective outlook, while the Renaissance in protestant countries is to be associated to a larger degree with the development of individualism.

THE INDUSTRIAL REVOLUTION AND MARKET CONTROL

The present chapter is concerned with the change from handicraft industry to the modern factory system only with respect to the bearing of the change upon the growth

---

[15] The reformation is subject to a fundamental economic interpretation but the attempt to interpret it through immediate conflict of economic interests is extremely superficial. *Cf.* Loria, *Economic Foundation of Society*, Garner translation, p. 372.

of market control over economic affairs. Toynbee identified the industrial revolution with the establishment of a free market.[16] One scarcely could do worse in interpreting the development of market control. Such a revision of economic institutions is not an industrial fact. To make the establishment of the market a revolution minimizes centuries of slow development. One might just as well say that the breaking of an egg shell constitutes the hatching of a chick. Furthermore, such a characterization of the revolution removes it from the field of technical methods to the field of institutional organization. On all counts it appears better to leave the term its usual meaning of a change of technological processes.

Parenthetically, the figure of a hatching chick is peculiarly descriptive of what happened to the market at the time of the industrial revolution. The revolution did break a great deal of shell away from the market—more in some countries than in others. Through its improvements of transportation and its tremendous increase of industrial output the revolution brought a great change in the size and extent of markets and in the number and variety of goods marketed. In fact, the revolution completed the job of establishing the market as the authoritative machinery for the adjustment of ordinary conflicts of economic interests. But economic control by the market can not by any stretch of the

[16] "The essence of the Industrial Revolution is the substitution of competition for the mediæval regulations which had previously controlled the production and distribution of wealth." *Industrial Revolution*, p. 85.

imagination be made a product of the revolution. The market was rather an outgrowth of circumstances prevailing in the handicraft period. As we shall see in the following chapter, the revolution brought into play factors which were antagonistic to the market. Although the immediate effect of the revolution was to establish the market more firmly than ever before in its seat of authority, the more characteristic and more fundamental effect of the revolution has been its undermining of market control.

A recent book on modern European economic history gives an excellent account of commercial developments antecedent to the industrial revolution.[17] It presents a convincing argument for the view that modern business enterprise and modern economic expansion came before the industrial revolution and were controlling factors in shaping the development of the revolution. This view makes the industrial revolution an incidental feature of the modern economic development of Western peoples.

However, the authors of the book here mentioned tend to make a prime mover of the development of commerce, or capitalism or business enterprise. They give an account of its growth but do not account for its development. They minimize the significance of the Renaissance and Reformation by dubbing them "dramatic but incidental factors in a general situation." By implication the growth of commerce is left as more than an incidental factor in a general situation. This tendency

[17] Knight, Barnes and Flügel, *Economic History of Europe in Modern Times.*

to accept commercial development as a prime mover is responsible, perhaps, for their following Professor Hayes in his use of the somewhat forced title, "The Commercial Revolution," for their chapter dealing with commercial expansion during the centuries immediately preceding the industrial revolution.[18]

The writer has no quarrel with the authors here criticised over their description of the relationship between commercial developments and the industrial revolution. The protest here expressed is an objection to bestowing upon commercial developments the rôle of prime mover which very properly is taken away from the industrial revolution. It is argued herein that the commercial expansion antecedent to the industrial revolution was an incidental factor in a general cultural situation along with the Renaissance and the Reformation. It is suggested further that the handicraft industrialism of Northern Europe was a conditioning factor which contributed

[18] *Cf.* The following passage from page 301:
"What the commercial revolution overturned—or rather finished overturning—was the mediæval system of society, with its hierarchy of guilds, its more or less isolated manors and villages, its town units in commerce, its notions of just price and condemnation of interest and profits, and its comparatively meager trade along generally north-and-south lines, financially dominated from the Mediterranean northward. Perhaps most important of all was the overthrow of the stereotyped social order, and the recognition that the creative power of a myriad of personal ambitions is susceptible of some control. It is dangerous, like all great forces but it was always so to the lower classes. Modern European society has gradually released it, dubbed it personal initiative in its chastened and approved form, and attempted regulation."

largely to the shaping of this cultural situation in which modern business enterprise or modern capitalism achieved its phenomenal growth.

The objection may perhaps be offered that the view here expressed makes a prime mover of handicraft technology. And perhaps it does do so in form. But surely no one will doubt that such handicraft industrialism is itself subject to historical interpretation which would make it an incidental feature of the general process of cultural development. All that the present writer has to say on that score is that he has neither the resources nor the interest to undertake such an interpretation of handicraft industry.

OTHER FACTORS AFFECTING DEVELOPMENT OF MARKET CONTROL

While it is true that market control is dependent in large measure upon individualistic habits, whose roots go back to handicraft industry and increasing commercial development, nevertheless numerous other factors are to be taken into account. Development of the free market was a conjuncture of various influences. During those centuries when individual freedom was developing, that is, when there was being developed a set of habits which we describe by saying that they represent freedom of individual initiative, other changes were taking place. It was a period of rapid development in many lines, particularly in its later stages. The growth of new religious movements, the revolution of political theory and the expansion of the political unit in national development, geographic exploration and colonization, a rapid increase of production and trade, the improvement of printing with its attendant effects; all were significant features of the period in which free competition was developing. An outstanding characteristic of the period was expansion. Such a period of growth and expansion tends to promote individual action. The presence of a frontier is always an invitation to freedom. It tends, thereby, to prevent the economic oppression of any class. Conditions incident to economic and cultural expansion were, therefore, favorable to the development of a general policy of laissez faire. The market acquired its position of dominant authority because it fitted into the prevailing situation. Circumstances made it an effective tool. The mere fact that a free play of economic interests worked well when it was tried, tended strongly to establish more wide-spread confidence in the market.

Describing, then, in its largest aspects, the development of market control over economic affairs, we can say that it rested upon the following:

1. The independent, individualistic viewpoint of a non-feudal merchant class.

2. Development of the trader's viewpoint into a common philosophy of individualism, a development which is to be credited largely to a favorable discipline afforced by handicraft industrialism.

3. The conjuncture of this discipline with various other factors favorable to the spread of individualistic habits; a situation in which the market proved a particularly useful and appropriate piece of machinery.

WHEN MARKET CONTROL ARRIVED

As above indicated, the final chapter in the establishment of the free market was the industrial revolution. The revolution increased transportation facilities enormously and correspondingly increased production through quantity production of machine made goods. It increased greatly both the number of markets and the scope of particular markets. Its immediate effect therefore was to make more nearly universal the market's control over economic affairs.

Nevertheless, a competitive régime was in operation in England prior to the industrial revolution there. It has been asserted that the competitive system was centuries in developing. To name a particular date for its establishment would therefore infer a denial of the evolutionary process involved. But this does not mean it is not worth while to point out different circumstances and different stages of the process. For practical purposes we might well select a time which would serve better than any other as a distinguishing mark between the competitive system and its antecedents. Such a dividing line is afforded in England by the absorption of the law merchant into the common law.

Trading for profit was destined to be the foundation of a new order. It could not be the basis of an economic system so long as trading was limited to a special class of those economically active. When freedom of contract became potentially and theoretically universal, a system of law for merchants outside of the common law was no longer applicable to the situation. The logic of circumstances forced an incorporation of the law merchant into the common law. This change came in England during the sixteenth and seventeenth centuries.[19]

Two changes of especial interest are to be noted in the legal decisions of that period. One of these was to the effect that it was no longer necessary to be a merchant to enjoy certain legal privileges previously accorded only to merchants. The second, implied in the first, was that the law merchant was included in and part of the common law. Thus, according to this standard, we must say that as an actual fact of general economic organization around the market, the competitive system arose in England some two centuries before the appearance of a systematic body of theory describing such an organization.

SUMMARY

1. Town development was an important factor in the passing of the feudal régime of northern Europe.

2. This development rested upon commerce and a growth of handicraft industrialism. It was handicraft industrialism which turned the tide of economic and political development in favor of North European countries.

3. Critics of the guilds, like Gross, bitterly attack

[19] Holdsworth, *A History of English Law,* Vol. V., pp. 145-146. Holdsworth cites a case dating back to 1543 in which it was declared that the law merchant was part of the common law. However, general acceptance of this principle was a matter of slow development.

them for their restraints upon freedom of economic action. Such an attitude tends to contrast them with the later developed open market situation. An unbiased appraisal would contrast them with both the later situation and the feudal order. Guild-controlled handicraft represents a station between the feudal régime and the open market.

4. Growth of commerce taken alone produced the "bourgeois" merchant prince. Commerce plus handicraft industrialism produced the modern democratic or individualistic cultural period.

5. One feature of the development of an individualistic cultural period was the evolution of a competitive system of economic organization.

6. Introduction of a machine technology served to break down many anachronistic restrictions upon freedom of economic action; increased the scope of the market, and gave it a position of dominance it had not before occupied.

7. However, the market had become a focal point of actual and general economic organization in England some two centuries before the industrial revolution there.

CHAPTER IV
DISINTEGRATION OF MARKET CONTROL

The present chapter is not to be a study, especially, of institutional degeneration. It will be confined to a discussion of factors tending to bring about a decline of popular faith in market control.

As before stated, the chief cause accounting for the displacement of a given social order is the development of a new order. Such a decisive factor may be termed positive as against certain negative factors or causes tending to eliminate the old order without having direct, positive relation to the new. The opportunity for such a distinction between positive and negative factors arises from the fact that we must deal with fragmentary complexes of causes. If we could make a thoroughgoing objective analysis the distinction would lose its significance. But in the present state of our comprehension of social phenomena, the distinction may stand.

In historical analyses, looking back upon social changes, positive factors necessarily loom large and are rightly accorded the dominant consideration. But when a change is in progress or in prospect, a forward-looking analysis cannot follow the lines of the historical perspective. The so-called negative factors must of necessity occupy a disproportionate amount of the picture in any close-up view of current cultural changes.

The process of a general cultural change is in a sense

relatively negative in its earlier stages. Men lose faith in given institutions before they discard them—sometimes long before. They lose faith in them as actual social machinery before they lose faith in them as social ideals. Thus institutional machinery which becomes an object of attack is first criticised and condemned upon grounds of the philosophy and ideals with which its origin was associated. Practical action arising from such criticism takes the form of attempts to restore to institutions criticised their earlier effectiveness in meeting the requirements of social adjustment. If the machinery at stake is such a vital part of the social organization as the market, representing as it does the very foundation of our economic order, the disintegration of general confidence in it is very slow. When, however, changing circumstances do eventually undermine confidence in such an institution, the exigencies of practical affairs impel those who have lost faith in it to transfer their trust to other machinery in which they do have confidence. In practice they do not all transfer their trust to the same machinery. The result is a period of conflicting authorities.

Such a period of conflict our culture is now experiencing. We have business organizations with which the government negotiates and comes to terms, as illustrated in some trust prosecutions. We have labor organizations welded together in a hierarchy which constitutes a state within a state. These are outstanding examples of conflict between economic and political authorities. There are now many unadjusted conflicts between economic groups, but at such a time as the present the conflict between economic classes is merely an outstanding example of a general condition of irritation and conflict between authorities of many kinds.

PLURALISM IN POLITICAL THEORY

In political science, whose special province it is to discuss authorities, a condition of conflict has been indicated in recent years by discussions of the notion of a pluralistic state. In such discussions of pluralism in government it has been shown that pluralism is at times inevitable and that it is nothing new; that political monism may well develop out of political pluralism. For example the following:

"The fact is that in the early history of federal government there was no principle upon which a monistic American state could be said to rest. That principle was the creation of fifty years of political development and experience. Why should a political theory be compelled to assume, in defiance of the facts, that every juristic development takes place instantaneously, by some process analogous to the promulgation of an authoritative decree." [1]

The monistic authority which is here pictured as having developed during the first fifty years of United States history has more or less disintegrated during the last fifty years of that history.

Speaking more directly of the present situation and the

[1] G. H. Sabine, "Pluralism, a Point of View," *American Political Science Review*, Vol. 17, p. 34.

PLURALISM IN POLITICAL THEORY

prospect of a new political unity, Professor Sabine continues as follows: "How long this loose-ended state of affairs can last, or whether it can ever be fully supplanted by authoritative juristic means for defining jurisdictions, is a matter for speculation. The process will go on, if at all, not because of the desire for a consistent juristic theory but because conflicts are inconvenient, and in any case it cannot go faster than effective limits of jurisdiction can be found and effective authorities developed."

Referring later to agreement between authorities in a pluralistic state, he says, "Such agreement has in fact to be reached by the interchange of opinion, the compromise of differences, and the harmonization of interests—in short by negotiation."

Put these statements together; add the assumption of a common fundamental viewpoint, and the result is a description of conditions necessary to development of a new situation of simplicity and unity. Such an outcome is envisaged in the personal program with which Professor Sabine closes his discussion as follows: "For my own part, then, I must reserve the right to be a monist when I can and a pluralist when I must."

In other words, government is an evolutionary process. At times the duties and functions of governing authorities are relatively clear cut, simple and consistent. But at other times the presence of unadjusted conflicts sets at naught the simple theory of a monistic, sovereign state. This, as political theory, is parallel to the economic theory of alternating periods of adjustment and conflict between social institutions and their underlying economic setting. As a believer in economic interpretation would perhaps say, it is the political manifestation of economic determinism.

PRESENT TOPIC ECONOMIC DISORGANIZATION

In a later connection the prospect for a new political unity will be discussed further. The present chapter is concerned solely with the negative side of cultural changes now in progress. Specifically, the present task is to enumerate certain factors which have tended to destroy confidence in the market as an authoritative instrument of economic control and thereby have helped to bring about the pluralistic state of affairs in which we now find ourselves; a general state of affairs of which political conditions and economic conditions are only fractional parts.

The discussion of the present chapter, for the most part, will be limited in its application to the United States. An earnest conviction that control by competition has not worked out to equitable results is at the basis of a decline of faith in market control. To put the matter in a sentence men have lost faith in market control because they have come to believe it has worked out to their harm. This dissatisfaction is to be explained in terms of a changing economic system. It means merely that new times have brought new economic and social problems.

CHANGED CONDITIONS OF COMPETITIVE CONTROL

The conditions surrounding competitive control have changed greatly during the progress of its development. When competition became the rule in Great Britain and in the American colonies, the prevailing unit of competition was the individual. Through a process which was greatly stimulated by the industrial revolution, markets have become dominated by competitive units which include large groups of individuals. Some of these units, such as the corporation, have arisen through legal authorization; some, like trade unions, remain by legal tolerance, and others, like trusts dissolved in name but not in fact, remain in spite of legal opposition. By the sophisticated reasoning of trained economists, the market still is presented as the arbiter of individual interests, but the process of such adjustment is not obvious to one not so trained. The market has become far too large and complex for realistic description in individualistic terms.

The mere fact of the size and complexity of the market has not itself created an attitude of distrust. The effect of those characteristics has been merely to weaken the strategic position of market control by rendering it less obviously natural. Thereby the way has been opened for more active agencies of distrust.

LARGE SCALE COMPETITIVE PRODUCTION

Large competitive units engaged in the production of goods have tended to give the consumer a feeling of helplessness. If a consumer has thought a product too high in price there has been nothing he could do about it other than get along without that particular product. He could not undertake to produce the good himself and the chances are he has known no one who was in a position to do so. The producer has been to all intents and purposes a stranger to the consumer and subject to much of the suspicion and distrust which attaches to a stranger. Furthermore, market conditions induced by competitive production on a large scale have been such as to foster suspicion and distrust. Leaving aside for the moment all question of monopolistic and semi-monopolistic exploitation, the development of large scale production, with its large overhead organization and large overhead costs, typically has been accompanied by increased keenness of competition. The significance of successful production on a large scale has meant playing the game for larger stakes. In the effort to meet competition, producers frequently have lost sight of their costs, particularly overhead costs. It has been a common procedure to produce and sell below cost in order to stamp out injurious competition. The technique of management also has not kept pace with the growth of the competitive unit. Managers have not had adequate tools in the shape of accounting and statistical technique. As a result, the complexity of large scale productive processes frequently has reduced the control of managers to the plane of guesswork. This consequence has tended to create a certain amount of market instability. And, furthermore, the very size of the competitive unit has made it harder to initiate competition and harder for the unsuccessful competitor to drop out.[2]

The result of the foregoing considerations has been a more or less chronic state of maladjustment of production to the market. This has meant no profits to producers of particular goods for particular markets at some times and high profits at other times. It has meant also accompanying fluctuations in the prices of goods. Low prices due to keen competition have given the consumer

[2] It cannot be denied that consumption, and many prices also, have become more stabilized with the development of modern industrial technique. But such increasing stabilization does not contradict the argument here presented. When instability was the rule, when famines and times of plenty were looked upon as acts of God, it was not the part of piety to be dissatisfied with the ways of Providence. Economic stability was not to be expected or even thought of. Hence instability afforded no basis for dissatisfaction. But when economic instability came to be associated with and ascribed to the management of business enterprise a new basis for dissatisfaction with the existing economic order was introduced.

Of course there are malcontents in every generation. The present chapter is not concerned with the economic discontent of other periods but solely with grounds for discontent with the competitive market in the current economic situation.

It is not to be inferred that business management generally has deteriorated or that management of large scale business has been less able than that of small scale enterprise. In fact there has been steady improvement in the technique of management and undoubtedly the ablest managers have been attracted by large scale enterprises. Nevertheless, the problems of management have multiplied more rapidly than the technique of management has improved. Until very recently the development of accounting technique has not kept pace with the increasing complexity of productive operations.

a basis for comparison. Higher prices have therefore impressed him as excessive. So long as the consumer has been ignorant of the conditions of production the effect upon his psychology has been the same whether high prices were actually unreasonably high or low prices unreasonably low.

Such instability of competitive conditions is, of course, not surprising in the use of a comparatively new technology and one that has been developing rapidly. It has not been universal but it has happened frequently enough and upon a sufficient scale to justify emphasizing it has one of the factors undermining confidence in market control.

FROM CUT-THROAT COMPETITION TO MONOPOLY

Instability of large scale competitive production, such as that above described, has been a continual goad towards combination of business interests and still further growth of the productive unit. Growth of the producing unit to proportions which have enabled it to dominate single handed the markets served by it sometimes has made it possible for such a favored enterprise to correct the instability incident to large scale competitive production. In doing so, however, such enterprises have only made matters worse by running afoul of the law under charges of monopoly or conspiracy in restraint of trade. Monopolistic stability has been, doubtless, a more powerful disseminator of distrust than competitive instability. Spectacular "trust busting" activities of state and federal officials have been the means of crystallizing into definite convictions impressions which before were somewhat vague. The damning evidence of notorious cases, the persistent appearance of monopoly at different times, as well as its appearance in many different lines, and the continual inauguration of new campaigns against old or new trusts by zealous politicians, all have combined to give currency to the conviction, that, as a rule, big business dominates its markets rather than is controlled by them.

Thus fluctuating prices and instability of operating conditions which have accompanied a rapid development of large scale production have tended to create a popular conviction that regulation by competition is not working well. At the same time, this instability has tended to bring about a protective cooperation and an elimination of competition in many cases. But the cure, no less than the disease itself, has contributed to a further undermining of confidence in market control.

AGRICULTURAL DISTRUST

The presence of certain economic groups which are more or less self-conscious has contributed to distrust of actual markets. Members of the agricultural group, for example, commonly have come to the point of believing that they are beset on both sides by the trust evil. Observation that the prices of staple farm products fluctuate more than the prices of goods the farmer buys has been proof to the farmer that while one set of monopolies drives down the prices of what he has to sell, another set keeps up the prices of what he must buy. Prosecutions of the International Harvester Company on the one hand, and of meat-packing combinations on the other hand, for example, have in this case been the means of converting suspicion and discontent into positive conviction.

Agriculture has remained essentially a small scale industry, but it is one which always has suffered some of the ills of large scale manufacturing. The farmer has had at his disposal a relatively large investment of capital in land which could not profitably be left idle. His production has been guided with a view to keeping it in use. His output, as a whole, has been limited by the character of the season rather than by adjustment to market conditions. The business side of farming has, therefore, been subject to an instability and a disadvantage which are explainable in terms of the industry itself without recourse to monopolistic exploitation by other interests. However, the character of this explanation does not alter the case at all for present purposes. The actual situation has made the farmer suspicious of the markets he must patronize.

It is to be noted in this connection, however, that the influences which have led the farmer to distrust the markets in which he buys and sells, have not destroyed his adherence to the principles upon which market control rests. He still subscribes, as a rule, to the individualistic theory under which market control developed. The small scale character of his industry, his relative independence and the technological discipline of his occupation in the past have all tended to preserve such a point of view.[3]

THE LABOR POINT OF VIEW

Labor forms another group which is to be compared and in some respects contrasted with the agricultural group. Development of machine industry soon demonstrated the necessity for special protection of workers engaged in it. Protective legislation passed specially for their benefit has been increasing ever since the introduction of machine technology. The reason for this does not need development here. The relative weakness of the lone worker in a capitalistic system is obvious.

In addition to legislative protection, another form of assistance has been afforded industrial and craft workers in that they have been permitted to protect themselves through conspiracies in restraint of free competition. Trade unions are based upon cooperative or joint action against employers. Their working ideal is a satisfactory negotiation of trade agreements. Collective bargaining is fundamental to their existence. Thus their essence is an agreement to limit or rather, to destroy competition.

The development of such labor organizations to their present status has been possible only because both authorities in charge of them and the politically constituted authorities of the country have as a rule avoided legal

[3] There have been many other periods of agricultural revolt but that fact does not render the present revolt any less significant as a factor in the current situation.

conflicts whenever possible. The attitude of legal authority towards labor is in fact not essentially different from its attitude towards business management, or capital.[4] The difference is mainly a matter of form. The law has endeavored to preserve a fictitious individuality in the unit of business management. At the same time it has tolerated, in fact though not always in judicial precedent, labor conspiracies which have not even a pretense of individuality.

Labor authorities defend labor conspiracies upon the superficial pretext that labor service is not a commodity of sale. And the position of the law with respect to the labor contract lends some color to the pretext.[5] But, needless to say, legal tolerance of the labor conspiracy is not due to the efficacy of this pretext. It rests, rather upon a tacit recognition of the necessity for some such protection of the working class and a desire to avoid social consequences which would follow a contrary course of action.

Thus two important foundation stones of labor's present economic position are special protective legislation and a form of cooperative action. Both are in-

[4] The law has not always been consistent in its treatment of either labor or business enterprise. It has been somewhat more sympathetic in its treatment of business because the interests of business more neatly fit into an inherited legal system, but treatment of the two has been much more fundamentally similar than it has different. For differences, cf. Commons, *Legal Foundations of Capitalism*, Ch. VIII.

[5] Cf. Commons, *op. cit.*

fringements upon the principle of market control through competition.

A fundamental reason for the antagonism of labor groups to market control is the fact that the discipline of machine industry upon the workers in it is such as to engender habits of thought inconsistent with those fostered by the earlier discipline of handicraft industry.[6] The logic of the free market presented in Chapter III does not strike the factory worker as reasonable. In point of fact, it is not intelligible to him. To his limited comprehension it is merely part of the employer's strategic equipment along with the courts which go to such pains in enforcing it.

The crux of the so-called labor problem lies in the fact that the labor group, almost entirely, has lost faith in the existing economic system, that is, in control by competition. Those groups of workers who are least highly organized, but nevertheless class conscious, are, as a rule, most outspoken in their antagonism towards the existing régime because their lot is harder and they have less at stake in the way of recognized rights and privileges. But the highly skilled craftsman and the relatively unskilled syndicalist are alike hostile to the principle of control by free competition.[7]

[6] Hoxie, "The Trade Union Point of View," *Journal of Political Economy*, Vol. 15, p. 345.

[7] This statement represents the views of craftsmen rather than an official position of the A. F. of L. Members of those highly skilled groups which are associated in the A. F. of L. are intensely antagonistic to the appearance of individualistic or competitive

EFFECTS OF GOVERNMENT REGULATION

Enumerating the above-mentioned factors tending to undermine market control, we have, the increased size of the market and of the competitive unit, a characteristic instability of competitive production on a large scale, development of the so-called capitalistic monopolies and certain special influences affecting the agricultural and labor groups of the population.

Still another factor contributing to the same end is government control of public utilities—the "natural monopolies." Such regulation by both state and national governments is a firmly established practice. A significant feature of this regulation is the fact that it touches so large a proportion of the population at so many points. Patrons of such services are brought to look to the gov-

---

actions within their ranks. Even in the official policy of the A. F. of L. it is not possible to find a defense of regulation by competition. An insistence upon craft organization and action is not a defense of competition. If pickpockets and holdup men agreed to organize separately and to operate as independent groups, we would not conclude that they therefore advocated competition among thieves. The fact that the two groups exploited the same people would not make them competitors within the technical meaning of that term.

Of course labor groups protest against lack of competition among business interests. But that also is an example of opportunist tactics. A realistic labor slogan would be "Competition by employers; cooperation by employees."

The A. F. of L. offers no ideal of economic or social organization. Its wholly opportunist character is well indicated by testimony of labor leaders before the United States Industrial Commission 1898-1901.

EFFECTS OF GOVERNMENT REGULATION

ernment rather than to a competitive market for their protection with reference to railroad rates, telephone and telegraph rates, gas, water and electric current rates, to mention only some of the most common examples. And the important consideration for present purposes is not the fact of public regulation but the change from market regulation to government regulation and the clash of interests which has been responsible for the change. An outright government monopoly like the mail service might exist indefinitely without having any appreciable effect upon the prevailing attitude towards a general dependence upon market control. But if the mails were at first privately managed and, as a result of injustices incident to such management, the government should take them over, the change would tend to have a distinct effect which predetermined government management does not have. Thus regulation is important both because of the increasing number of things regulated and because of the fact of change from market regulation to government regulation. Incidentally, government regulation affects most intimately that class of consumers which in popular parlance is the backbone of social stability—the stable middle class.

An examination of the development of government regulation throws still further light upon its importance for our present purposes. Regulation uniformly has begun in a negative, restrictive fashion. A government agency has been called in to supplement market control in a particular field. Gradually the government agency has been impelled by the logic of successive decisions to formulate and enforce a more and more positive program of control. With respect to public service enterprises, market control has retired from the field as government control has become more and more positive. This shift has been a gradual process. Its sanction and support by legislative authority has been dependent upon a gradual change of public opinion. (Such a line of development has been strikingly illustrated in the case of the Interstate Commerce Commission and it is to be traced also in the various fields of state regulation.) It is this gradual shift of public opinion which is important to the present argument. Regulatory acts which would not have been countenanced fifty years ago now receive practically unanimous support. And since regulated enterprises are numerous, affecting a large percentage of the population at many points of each individual's everyday life, the change has been a potent influence bearing upon the individual's reaction towards the fundamental principle of market control.

THE BUSINESS CYCLE

Notwithstanding the general significance of the foregoing points of argument, they have run in terms of special incidence only. Particular groups of the population have been affected or particular lines of business enterprise have been involved. There remains to be presented another point of argument which runs in terms of the current economic régime as a whole.

In spite of the prevalence of conflicting points of view and a wide divergence of class interests, the mechanism of the current economic organization shows a remarkable coherence and unity. Modern technology has developed the principle of division of labor to such a point that machine industry no longer means merely the independent use of power-driven machines. Our entire economic system has taken on the characteristics of a vast machine.[8]

The development of a coherent industrial organization is only one aspect of the existing economic system. Another aspect is the development of corresponding machinery of control. Business management and technological operations have come to be relatively distinct but complementary parts of a single system. Their relations will call for discussion later. Our present interest is in the one relation of business control over industry through the machinery of credit.

Business credit is not a product of modern business. It merely grew greatly when conditions became favorable for its growth. All that has been written upon the business cycle in recent times has its outstanding significance in its proof that large parts of our economic system operate as a unit, that is, there is a cycle or rhythm in business activity. And the essential conclusion to be drawn from a study of the cycle is the one that it is a product of the credit market—a result of dependence upon a competitive control of credit. In other words the business cycle is a form of economic instability which results from a dependence upon market control in a highly developed credit economy of the current type.

[8] Veblen, *Theory of Business Enterprise,* Ch. II..

It is needless to emphasize here the fact that the essential unity of the current régime is not a product of business foresight. It has resulted from countless tentative and sometimes abortive movements of business enterprise; from movements which are of the same stripe as those which characterize the evolution of so-called natural phenomena. Coherence and unity have resulted from their survival value. With all due respect to particular captains of industry and lords of finance, both their constructive contributions and their criminal responsibilities have been greatly exaggerated. The great man theory of political history meets with a great deal of skepticism on the part of modern historians. The economic historian has every reason to be similarly skeptical as to the influence of particular individuals.

However, the development of coherent, unified economic machinery has meant that certain individuals, or groups of individuals, inevitably have been thrown into strategic positions which have multiplied their importance and power incalculably.[9] And when those who occupy such positions may take advantage of their strategic power to profit by the economic instability of the business cycle, it is not surprising that they should be charged with manipulation of the cycle. Such charges notwithstanding, the business cycle is not a product of monopolistic control, not even of a monopoly of credit, not even of a "money trust." It is a product of the competitive use and control of credit. And the freer the play of competitive

[9] *Cf.* W. C. Mitchell, *Business Cycles, The Problem and Its Setting*, pp. 169-173.

forces in the credit market, the greater the violence of the resulting economic instability.

Thus the business cycle is the crowning example of the failure of competition to produce economic stability. Competition has not only failed in particular lines where special conditions prevail: at the same time it has failed signally in a much larger sense. Under its supposed control the whole business régime has periodically run amuck.[10]

The influence of this major failure of the market, in undermining confidence in market control, has been multiplied by the fact that congressional investigations, political oratory of candidates for office, and attacks of socialistic propagandists frequently have dramatized it around conspicuous financial personages. In any appraisal of factors tending to destroy confidence in market control, the instability involved in the business cycle takes first place both because of its fundamental importance and because of the publicity it has received.

UNCERTAINTY OF LEGAL SUPPORT

Finally, the market has lost prestige because of a defection of legal support. When the law permits continued existence of conspiracies in abrogation of competition; when the supreme court of the United States has been jockeyed by public opinion and the force of circumstances into taking a position which makes it virtually a semi-administrative board of censorship over the activi-

[10] *Cf.* W. C. Mitchell, *Business Cycles, The Problem and Its Setting*, pp. 169-173.

ties of big business;[11] when a trial judge can say, "The higher courts nowadays decide so many things upon a basis of public policy that no one can tell by law what the outcome of a given case will be;" when legislatures and courts from time to time give sanction to new inroads upon private property, then even the support of the law, which is supposed to surround and protect control by the open market, appears to be breaking down.

PRESENT POSITION OF THE MARKET

The origins of law lead back to common fundamental beliefs, to general principles or ideals to which adherence was given by the people among whom the body of law in question was developed.[12] It does not follow from this, however, that a system of legal rules ceases to function as soon as its fundamental foundation loses the support of a majority of the people. Since positive adherence of the mass of the people constitutes the process of election of new principles, old rules hold over until their successors are duly selected. And so it is also with institutions like the market. In spite of the whittling away from its authority by government regulation; in spite of influences which have undermined and often destroyed entirely the confidence of major groups of the population in it, the market still stands as part of the larger social order of which representative government is itself a part. In the eyes of the law and theoretical

[11] M. W. Watkins, "The Change in Trust Policy," *Harvard Law Review*, Vol. 35, p. 815.
[12] Bruce Wyman, *Control of the Market*, p. 1.

economics, the market still stands as the central, supreme economic authority. But it stands thus without the loyal support of a large majority of those who are subject to its faltering control.

SUMMARY

1. While historical analysis permits an emphasis upon positive or constructive development of particular cultural periods, a forward-looking analysis of the passing of an old régime necessarily lays more stress upon negative factors involved.

2. The existing cultural situation is one of more than ordinary transition—a period of conflict and disorganization. This condition is indicated in political organization by current discussions of the notion of a pluralistic state. In economics it is typified by a general decline of faith in market control.

3. The modern market has become so large and complex that a realistic analysis of it is no longer possible in individualistic terms. Its growth to such proportions has opened the way for a distrust of market control.

4. The development of large scale competitive production has been characterized by an instability of prices and profits. This has promoted discontent because of its being ascribed to the management of those in control of industry.

5. Resulting vicissitudes of competitive production, in conjunction with other causes, have led to the formation of capitalistic monopolies. Such monopolies have further stimulated a distrust of the market.

84 DISINTEGRATION OF MARKET CONTROL

6. Certain special conditions have tended to foster distrust among members of the agricultural and labor groups. The labor group has even become actively hostile to the principle of control by competition.

7. A rapid increase of government regulation has been supported by a distinct change of public opinion relative to such a policy. The change from market regulation to government regulation is especially important as both indicating and promoting a changed point of view.

8. The business cycle is the crowning example of instability under a competitive régime. Competition has failed with respect to some very important lines of economic activity. At the same time it has failed to afford reasonably efficient control over the existing economic system as a whole.

9. The legal system which developed along with the development of market control is itself disintegrating. Thereby the vitality of the market is greatly impaired.

10. So strong have been the influences undermining the market that, while it still stands in a nominal position of authority, it is no longer effectively authoritative.

CHAPTER V

THE DECADENCE OF VALUE THEORY

Time was when economics, or political economy, was a general system of theory dealing with the mechanism of economic organization. In the hands of the different schools of value theorists, the subject dealt in an avowedly superficial manner with the competitive market while purporting to present more fundamental theories of value and distribution.

However, the modern stress upon specialization and division of labor has made itself felt in academic circles as elsewhere. It has wrought havoc upon the early unity of the college course in political economy. Courses in theory have remained as a sort of parent stock while numerous progeny have appeared as courses in money and currency, banking, international trade, foreign and domestic exchange, transportation, public finance, corporation finance and labor. At the same time other more or less illegitimate children have made their appearance as courses in accounting, industrial management, salesmanship, insurance, business statistics, business law, real estate, and many others.

Growth of the economics family has given rise to the problem of the relation of parent to offspring. Some have taken the position that in the teaching of economics, specialized instruction should be offered only as advanced courses in each of which the purpose should be to show how the principles of economic theory are illustrated and adapted, or modified, in that particular sphere of economic activity.[1] Such presumably, was the basis upon which specialized courses were introduced into college curricula.

However, the teachers of specialized courses have disclosed a persistent tendency to introduce their special subjects by means of courses which are essentially elementary. Such courses tend to draw upon the concrete facts of current economic affairs rather than upon a previous training of the student in economic theory. In so far as this tendency has been followed it represents a forsaking of the grounds upon which the specialized course was first introduced.

The condition here referred to has not been conducive to peace and happiness in the economics family. Those who have been inclined to insist upon "economic theory," as a basis for all specialized study in economics, have been prone to protest against "the multiplication of so-called practical courses." They have sometimes even intimated in private that the reason for elementary courses in the special subjects is a lack of scholarly training in economic theory on the part of teachers in those subjects.

Specialists who do not take kindly to the old-fashioned economic theory have returned the compliment passed upon them by inferring that the self-styled economic theorist belongs in a class with the school men of the

[1] *Cf.* statements made in a review by H. G. Brown in the *Quarterly Journal of Economics*, Vol. 36, pp. 331-2.

Middle Ages. Their view is neatly expressed by Prof. Gustav Cassel as follows:

"In my economic studies I long ago reached the conclusion that all the old value theory so-called, with its endless terminological controversies and its fruitless scholasticism, is superfluous ballast of which economic theory must rid itself." [2]

In some institutions this family quarrel takes the form of an issue between a department of economics and a department or school of business administration. Members of departments of "theoretical economics" are prone to look upon the business school as a trade school with aims patterned after those of the so-called commercial or business college. The department of economics in the arts college is held to stand for *ex parte* investigation or perhaps a study of economic affairs with an eye to group welfare.[3]

The business school cannot allow such a contrast to stand. Like other professional schools, the business school must rest its case upon group welfare rather than upon a conferring of benefits upon individuals trained by it. And if the business school assumes this social responsibility which alone justifies its existence, then the most fundamental *ex parte* investigation possible neces-

[2] *Theoretische Sozialökonomie*, p. 5. The above quotation is taken from "An Extension of Value Theory," by David Friday in the *Quarterly Journal of Economics*, Vol. 36, p. 197.

[3] *Cf.* Wallace B. Donham, "Investigation and Teaching of Social Aspects of Business," *Proceedings, Ninth Annual Meeting of the American Association of Collegiate Schools of Business.*

sarily becomes the chief instrument by which its purposes are to be accomplished. Thus, if the business school serves its function, it cuts the ground from under departments maintained to afford an independent discipline in economics. Under these circumstances it becomes a responsibility of the business school to make a careful appraisal of "economic theory" and to settle definitely the family quarrel about it.

DEFINING ECONOMIC THEORY

Students of economics do not agree in their usage of the term economic theory. Neither do their theoretical formulations admit of a neat classification. Nevertheless, something may well be gained by setting up distinct conceptions of economic theory without trying to classify particular individuals under one or another of the different definitions.

The reaction against traditional methods expressed in the above quotation from Professor Cassel suggests that economic theory should be so purged that its only remaining content would be an inductive, objective, statistical analysis of current economic affairs; including of course the use of whatever past statistical data are available. Such a view rids itself of all subjective difficulties at a stroke. The subject matter which it selects is definite and concrete. Adoption of this viewpoint results in a thoroughly scientific procedure. Quantitative measurement is rendered possible by a rigid adherence to the narrow limits of the chosen viewpoint.

Study from such a viewpoint cannot achieve the com-

DEFINING ECONOMIC THEORY

pleteness of a static deductive system. Neither can it be particularly evolutionary in its outlook. Its narrowness precludes a long time perspective.

At an opposite pole from the foregoing, stands the view that economic theory is synonymous with value and distribution theory of the traditional types. This view makes economic theory a subjective analysis of human conduct underlying, or constituting, competitive economic institutions. It gives rise to a closely logical system of theory set up primarily by deductive reasoning processes. Those inclined to this view do not question the value of work from the first viewpoint. They merely consider it too narrowly restricted to aspire to the title economic theory and they would give it another name.

The two foregoing conceptions are mutually exclusive. A third view represents at least a nominal attempt to bring them together by including both types of discussion under the one title economic theory. According to this third view both objective and subjective methods are to be used without prejudice to either one. However, this impartiality as to methods is not put into practice. (It cannot be and result in any consistent or significant body of theory.) Hence the nominal character of the attempt at amalgamation. The result is that those who profess this broader use of the term economic theory tend to cling to the established unity of a deductive system. They admit the propriety of inductive investigation, even within the theoretical field, but they know in advance, in a general way, what the results of any investigation ought to be. If in any given case the results obtained do not agree with fundamental principles, so much the worse for the statistics.

Still a fourth view would include in economic theory a study of the development of economic institutions, that is the development of systems of such institutions, and also the relation of economic institutions to other institutions. According to this view the operation of a particular scheme of economic institution is only a very small part of the field to be covered by economic theory.

The distinct feature of this fourth conception is its adoption of an evolutionary perspective. Thereby economics becomes, essentially, a study of cultural development from an economic standpoint.

With reference to method, this last conception is a reverse of the third view, which in practice has made objective procedure subordinate to a subjective analysis. In this last variety of theory the controlling viewpoint is objective but a subordinate use of the subjective method is necessary, at least in our present state of knowledge, in order to facilitate an evolutionary analysis. The relations of economic institutions to other institutions cannot now be expressed in objective terms.

It will be observed that this classification of conceptions of economic theory is based entirely upon method. Their characteristic features are respectively, the objective viewpoint or method, the subjective viewpoint or method, a predominance of the subjective over the objective and a predominance of the objective over the subjective.

Discussions under the first three run in definite, satisfying terms. Under the first, the use of a quantitative method affords definiteness. Under the second and third, definiteness is afforded by the logical procedure followed. But discussion along the line of the fourth conception necessarily is given over to relatively loose-ended generalizations. On this score, however, it might be said for the fourth view that it outlines a large field for exploitation by those whose work is in accordance with the first definition. It affords scope for the exercise of such imagination as is requisite to all pioneering scientific work.

AN APPRAISAL OF VALUE THEORY

Clearly the market mechanism is not an ultimate of social organization. An appeal from the market organization to something more fundamental is therefore entirely legitimate. In the third chapter of this discussion, the market, in its modern rôle, was presented as the economic aspect of a particular type of cultural organization. The strength of the market mechanism, as machinery of economic adjustment, was held to be dependent upon its coordination with other social institutions in a unified cultural scheme. The cultural situation which gave rise to the modern market mechanism, it was contended, was dominated by an individualistic or subjective viewpoint which shaped the development of a unified cultural scheme. The watchwords of that period were freedom, liberty, private property, personal religious faith and other slogans expressive of the dominant trend of thought characteristic of the period. This descriptive account of market development constitutes an appeal from the market mechanism to a broader cultural mechanism of which the market was itself a part.

In contrast with the foregoing interpretation, value theorists have not appealed to a broader mechanism. They have accepted objective, descriptive accounts of market operations as satisfactory, as far as they go, but have held such accounts to be necessarily superficial. They have not attempted to extend the scope of such objective descriptions but have sought to re-interpret market phenomena in subjective terms.

It need hardly be repeated here that the objective and subjective viewpoints are not thus reducible to common terms. And if not, the effort to pass from the one to the other by logical procedure is hopeless.

However, the efforts of the value theorists here referred to are not to be disposed of in any such summary fashion. The objective and subjective viewpoints are so intimately associated in our everyday life that they frequently are not clearly distinguished. For example, we may well say that one man is more patriotic than another. Patriotism, of course, is not something to be measured, or weighed or counted. It is not reducible to a quantitative concept. There are no units of patriotism. And yet it means something which is generally understood, to say that one man is more patriotic than another. If the country goes to war one man may be anxious to subscribe to "liberty loans" and may take a leading part in inducing others to do likewise while another man may require urging before he subscribes at all. When we say that the one man is more patriotic than the other we carry over into the realm of the subjective a quantitative form of speech which arises and belongs in the jurisdiction of the objective. When so used, such an expression becomes a mere figure of speech. No objection can be offered to it so long as it is clearly recognized as such.

Just as we can say that one man is more patriotic than another, so we can say that one good has more utility for us than another or one action more disutility than another. And upon this figure of speech value theories of the utility and disutility types are built.

THE NATURE OF THE ECONOMIC VALUE PROBLEM

The life of a group, like the life of an individual, may be organized subjectively or teleologically around different interests or ends. The problem of value is concerned with the fulfillment of these ends. Valuations may run in terms of either individual ends or group ends.

A theory of economic value is an interpretation of economic conduct. It relates economic conduct to conduct directed towards the fulfillment of other ends. When it fails to fulfill this function it is no longer valid. This idea has been well expressed and applied by Dr. David Friday as follows:

"Once we recognize that all valuation is purposive we have a test for the validity and sufficiency of any institution of pecuniary valuation like the market or the court sitting in a rate case. If the values which result from the working of these institutions function perfectly to realize the end which they are intended to serve they are true values. If not, the institutions which created them must be modified or supplemented by new ones."[4]

There is in this statement the clear implication that a theory of economic value must draw its validity from a particular scheme or ideal of social organization. It must rest upon social ends or values. And, in a sense, that is precisely what happened in the development of the pain cost, utility and utility *vs.* pain cost types of value theory.

Value theorists have held that they appealed from the market to a permanent and unchanging human nature. The claim never has been convincing. It is very much like the famous claim as to Eric the Red's discovery of America which is proved by the assertion that he sailed away and never came back. If he didn't go to America, where did he go?

However, the validity of the appeal involved in the above-mentioned types of value theory is not seriously impaired either by the fact that such theory is based upon the use of figurative language or by the minor error of value theorists in claiming an appeal to human nature. The appeal is, in fact, an appeal to a cultural philosophy underlying both the market and its coordinate institutions. Just as the philosophy of law rests a given system of law upon an underlying cultural philosophy so the types of economic value theory here under discussion served to rest the market mechanism of economic adjustment squarely upon the dominant philosophy of the period which gave rise to market control. In so doing they firmly established the market method of ad-

[4] David Friday, "An Extension of Value Theory," *Quarterly Journal of Economics*, Vol. 36, p. 197.

justment in the prevailing social organization and thereby justified a general governmental policy of laissez faire. They related economic conduct to other conduct by interpreting it in terms of the prevailing foundation of social organization. The fact that such value theory no longer serves this function of justification is not due to any inherent weakness in it but is due rather to the fact that both the economic mechanism and the cultural philosophy, which were associated with it, are being supplanted.

As the influence of a subjective cultural philosophy has waned, the justification rôle of value theory has become more and more out of date. Encouraged by their error with respect to its relation to human nature, economic theorists have continued defending value theory as a descriptive account of how the market is an outcome of interaction between human nature and an environment of economic resources, even while disclaiming it as a justification of a competitive régime.[5]

In this later defense of value theory, the figure of speech by which we say one good is more useful to us than another becomes more than a figure of speech. It comes to circulate as a statement of verifiable data in objective or quantitative terms. It is against this later aspect of value theory that the following criticisms of utility and value concepts are directed.

[5] *Cf.* "The Institutional Nature of Pecuniary Valuation." C. H. Cooley in the *American Journal of Sociology*, Jan., 1913. Professor Cooley presented a keen criticism of this particular error.

CRITICISMS OF VALUE THEORY

Things possess utility, or value in the subjective sense, because they are the means of accomplishing ends. But ends are themselves individualistic. There is no common denominator through which to measure them in comparable terms. They may be in conflict or may harmonize with each other, and they may or may not individually fit in with a larger program of ends, but they are not quantitatively comparable. On this account, it appears to the writer a mistake to use the term value except in a subjective sense. For example, the expression "quantity of value" is a contradiction in terms.

Value theory dwells overmuch upon the concept of choice between means. It often tends to ignore the fact that it is dealing always with the relationship of means to an end. As Doctor Friday says, "All valuation is purposive." In actual conduct choice is fundamentally a selection of ends. The problem of conduct is like the process of ordering a dinner from an extensive menu. We may be like a small boy and prefer desserts to other dishes but we do not therefore order ice cream, mince pie, pudding and cake. We do not select each dish on the basis of its separate and distinct appeal to our palate. Instead each is selected with a view to its relation to the rest and all of them together are selected in view of our other ends. If other persons are to dine with us, that may affect our ordering. What we expect to do afterward also may affect it. The problem is always one of coordinating immediate ends with others more remote.

CRITICISMS OF VALUE THEORY

If after dinner we debate whether to buy a book to take home and read, or a ticket to go to the theater, the choice to be made will not merely affect the next two or three hours. If we debate the matter intelligently each of the two proposed courses of action will be related hypothetically to our whole program of ends. No choice stands alone. Each is involved with numerous other choices. To blind ourselves to the complexity of the situation by saying that we compare the utility of the book with the utility of the theater ticket is, figuratively speaking, merely to stick our heads in the sand.

Utility is a concept resting upon subjective assumptions. The notion of its quantitative measurement gives it a pseudo objectivity which is quite illegitimate except as a figure of speech. This notion rests upon a confusion of objective and subjective assumptions. Nevertheless it has the standing which goes with long-continued and frequent repetition.

For a clear-cut criticism of this confusion and at the same time an illustration of it, the reader is referred to an article upon "Economic Value and Moral Value" by Prof. R. B. Perry.[6]

In his treatment of moral value Professor Perry is clear and incisive. "Moral value," he writes, "attaches to an act, motive or disposition viewed in the light of a rule or principle, which in turn is designed to organize and harmonize interests.—But the peculiar sort of principle which is in question in the moral life is that by which two or more interests otherwise conflicting may be

[6] *Quarterly Journal of Economics,* Vol. 30, p. 443.

brought into relations, at least of compatibility, if possible of cooperation and mutual reinforcement."

Value here clearly is concerned with the organization and harmonization of interests. The problem is not one of measurement but of organization and harmonization. But when it comes to economic value, Professor Perry does not live up to the logic of his assertion that all values "possess a generic sameness." Instead he surrenders to the traditional economic view that economic value is a measurable phenomenon and so generically different from the above conception of moral value. For example, the following:

"As to the measurement of the comparative strength of interests, it is only necessary, I think, to make this remark. Interests are matched directly against one another in the act of choice."

In answer to this, it is only necessary, I think, to make this remark. Interests are not matched directly against one another in the act of choice. Interests, to accept Professor Perry's term, do not present themselves in isolation from the problem of their harmonization. Not even economic interests. Choice is not a question of isolated alternatives but of selection from endless varieties or combinations of ends. Surely conduct involves the conflict or clash of moral issues in quite the same sense that it involves conflicts of economic interests; and frequently it involves both at the same time.

In criticism of the notion of a social value Professor Perry says, "To postulate a constant value for each commodity relative to society as a whole, and to substitute this for an analytical interpretation in terms of individuals as variables, seems to me to be neither hopeful nor sound. It is much as though one should propose to substitute a circular or elliptical force for the law of the parallelogram of forces by which such a force is analyzed into centrifugal and centripetal components."

And yet Professor Perry falls in with a precisely parallel error by which there is set up a measurable value, or utility, of goods to the particular individual. One might well paraphrase his own criticism as follows:

To postulate a measurable value of each commodity relative to a given individual and to substitute a hypothetical comparison of such values for an analytical interpretation of the individual's choice in terms of the various circumstances and influences bearing upon his action, seems to me to be neither hopeful nor sound. It is as though one should propose to substitute a circular or elliptical force for the law of the parallelogram of forces by which such a force is analyzed into centrifugal and centripetal components.

Doctor Friday's insistence that all valuation is purposive, keeps economic value in the field of organization and harmonization of ends. His statement is thus in direct line with Professor Perry's discussion of moral value. He accords economic value its proper place in the family of values, whereas Professor Perry's surrender to traditional economic theory makes an outcast of it.

Viewing from a purely objective point of view the circumstances to which the term utility is applied, we could use the term to report the fact that there are causes tending to bring about certain actions with reference to a given good. The term marginal utility might even serve to report that causes urging towards one line of action are balanced against one or several conflicting groups of causes. It could report a balanced conflict of tendencies without being in any way objectionable. But such usage would be distinctly outside the pale of that "internal" system of "subjective worths" set up by utility economists.[7]

To make the foregoing discussion specific with a familiar illustration, the housewife purchasing supplies is limited both by the offerings of the market and by the likes and dislikes of her family. Her son James may not like potatoes but nevertheless potatoes may play a con-

[7] *Cf.* Wicksteed, *Common Sense of Political Economy,* p. 76, and many other writers. The internal economy of the utility economists is a mythical sphere built upon the pattern of an external system of market prices. The notion of a common denominator and quantitative measurement within that internal economy is the fundamental delusion of the utility economist. It is no proof of such measurement to say that the individual does choose between different lines of possible action. That the individual does act and that his action bears directly upon the system of market prices cannot be disputed. But that there is a parallel adjustment in the external market and in an internal economy hypothecated for each individual is a gratuitous and highly questionable assumption. Adjustments in the market run in terms of price. The setting up of an objective common denominator for the influences bearing upon even one individual's conduct is not possible with our limited knowledge of human behavior. And the notion of setting up a subjective common denominator covering the individual's conduct or choice involves a philosophical contradiction. Subjective data are not amenable to expression in terms of equivalence.

siderable rôle in her dietetic schedule. James' repugnance to potatoes may cut some figure without being the sole determining factor involved. When the housewife's purchases of potatoes reach their marginal limit there are various causes or influences connected with the purchase of potatoes some of which are working for the purchase of more potatoes and others against it. The use of a single term to sum up the net result of all influences bearing upon the action of the housewife is, of course, perfectly legitimate provided that the term is truly descriptive. To sum up those influences and obtain a net or algebraic sum would require their separate measurement. Agreement to call this net result X, or utility, still leaves it an unknown term as long as the influences are not separately measured. Hence, when utility is conceived of as a common denominator of choices or ends or "interests" it becomes thereby a substitute for thought rather than a means of expressing an idea. It puts a damper upon clear thinking about the very relations which it purports to describe. It has been a useful tool in the interpretation of an economic situation which has not required its quantitative expression or measurement. But in a situation which requires exact economic adjustments it is no longer serviceable.[8]

[8] Professor Veblen presented a searching criticism of utility theory in "The Limitations of Marginal Utility," in *The Journal of Political Economy*, Vol. 17, p. 620. For example: "But while modern science at large has made the causal relation the sole ultimate ground of theoretical formulation, and while other sciences that deal with human life admit the relation of sufficient reason as a proximate, supplementary, or intermediate ground, subsidiary and subservient

102 THE DECADENCE OF VALUE THEORY

The term utility has no meaning apart from the relationship of means to an end. To be useful, a thing must be useful for something. However, economic activities of individuals frequently result from habit rather than from conscious reflection. It is true that the objective method cannot trace out all the myriads of antecedents or influences or causes bearing upon the simplest human choice. But neither can the subjective method forecast all the legion of consequences following upon such a choice. If it be admitted that conduct, or choice, is not fully controlled by conscious reflection, the utility theory encounters most serious difficulty. If reflection and habit are commonly involved in the same actions, the notion of a conscious comparison of utilities does not fit the situation.[9] If it be said that utility is broad enough to cover the case even though reflection does not, then utility comes to have a dual nature. A part of it, falling within the realm of reflective action, that is within the teleological interpretation of action, is clearly concerned with the relationship of means to an end. But the remainder, which is related to that portion of conduct which is not controlled by reflection, cannot have any

to the argument from cause to effect, economics has had the misfortune—as seen from the scientific point of view—to let the former supplant the latter." p. 626. This statement should be interpreted in the light of Veblen's own contention that the causal relation signifies a relation of equivalence. *Cf.* also "The Futility of Marginal Utility," by E. H. Downey in *The Journal of Political Economy*, Vol. 18, p. 253.

[9] This statement, for purposes of the argument, waives, in favor of the subjective analysis, the claim that reflection is habit.

concern with the relationship of means to an end; unless, to be sure, we say that the individual in question has unconscious ends towards the fulfillment of which is directed that portion of his conduct which is not controlled by reflection. Even if this last point be granted, the theory has reduced itself to an absurdity for thus it breaks down the very basis upon which the concept rests.

VALUE THEORY AND A NEW ECONOMIC THEORY

Critics of economic value theory do not all belong in one group by any means. One man flouts the notion that value theory is a fundamental interpretation of market phenomena but holds to price theory or market theory as essentially representative of the existing economic organization. Another man holds that market theory once was representative of the prevailing economic organization but is no longer so and that economic value theory never was other than a delusion.

The position taken in this discussion need not be repeated except to admit the tendency of the market mechanism to hold over beyond the period of dominance of the cultural philosophy with which it has been connected by value theory. However, social reorganization on the basis of a new viewpoint must carry with it the development of a new economic mechanism as well as a new cultural mechanism. It also must afford the eventual development of a new system of value theory to interpret a new economic situation.[10]

[10] *Cf.* Chapter XV below. The dependence of economic value theory upon a particular form or ideal of social organization is not

104 THE DECADENCE OF VALUE THEORY

Prof. Wesley C. Mitchell's presidential address before the American Economic Association was essentially a plea for a new economic theory.[11] He distinctly advocated a general appeal to the present concrete economic situation. Thus he is a leader of revolution in economics. His position on this score is not nullified by his diplomatic insistence that there is no present war among economists over the question of method. His repeated recognition of the fact that we cannot dispense with qualitative and subjective forms of thought and expression appears to be taken by some as a recantation of the position expressed in his presidential address and as a declaration on his part of allegiance to the current body of neo-classical economic theory.[12] This surely is not so. His work rests upon a shifting of dominant emphasis from the subjective to the objective and from the qualitative to the quantitative. And the carrying out of that

exceptional. Justification of economic institutions generally is dependent upon such an ideal. For example, the theory of property relates the institution to the accepted ideal. In the Middle Ages a devolution theory of social organization gave rise to a devolution theory or justification of property. The individualistic period gave rise to an individualistic or natural rights theory of property. Now the courts are muddling along with modifications of property rights based upon public policy. Their usage of the term public policy is a makeshift whereby they mark time until the appearance of a new social ideal gives them a new fundamental basis for the institution of property.

[11] *American Economic Review,* March, 1925.

[12] *Cf.* the above reference to the *American Economic Review (Supplement),* March, 1928.

VALUE AND ECONOMIC THEORIES 105

shift of emphasis involves a revolution in economic theory as it is taught in the United States.

When Professor Mitchell refers to his forthcoming second volume on Business Cycles, he says, "The cycles with which the discussion will deal are neither the cycles of history nor the cycles of some speculative construction, but cycles of an intermediate order." [18]

How shall we interpret this assertion? If they are not to be the cycles of history, they must be abstractions drawn from the actual cycles he has studied. If they are such abstractions, they are the product of speculative construction. It appears, therefore, that they are to be cycles not of *some* speculative construction but of *another* speculative construction. And what is the difference between *some* and *another* speculative construction?

The only reasonable interpretation of Professor Mitchell's statement appears to be that he intends to stress his appeal to the facts in the construction of his cycles' theory. If the "old economic theory" fits the new facts well and good. But in case of doubt, the new facts are to be the controlling consideration. When theory and facts part company, he proposes to say, not "So much the worse for the statistics," but "So much the worse for the theory." And the difference between those two statements is the difference between conservatism and revolution.

Nothing is to be gained from a categorical statement as to the truth or falsity of utility or pain cost theories

[18] *Business Cycles, The Problem and Its Setting,* p. 469.

of value. Undoubtedly the essential features of such theories possessed a functional or constructive validity in the development of an individualistic, competitive, democratic cultural organization. But in the present situation they no longer enjoy that constructive validity. Their loss of vitality has brought about a temporary eclipse of value theory. This decadence of value theory is, however, only the decadence of a particular type of theory. The emergence of a new type of value theory awaits fuller development of the two cultural phenomena which will be connected by it, that is, a new mechanism of economic adjustment and a new cultural philosophy.

It already has been pointed out that economics is not alone at fault among the social sciences in exhibiting a confusion of objective and subjective assumptions. As the present argument proceeds, reasons will become apparent why emphasis of the objective viewpoint is urged. These reasons will not assume any ultimate validity of that viewpoint over the subjective point of view. It may possibly be that "The world—is such stuff as ideas are made of." [14] This discussion is concerned only with a relatively immediate cultural situation. It is not concerned with metaphysical speculation as to an ultimate constitution of the universe.

SUMMARY

1. In its origin economic value theory was an appeal to an underlying cultural philosophy and thereby it

[14] Royce, *The Spirit of Modern Philosophy*, p. 380.

served to justify the market method of economic adjustment.

2. As its rôle of justification has become obsolete, value theory has been preserved as a descriptive account of how the market mechanism results from interaction of human nature and an environment of economic resources.

3. This later day rôle of value theory rests upon a failure to distinguish objective and subjective concepts —a failure to recognize that figurative language is figurative.

4. The problem of conduct is a problem in the harmonization and coordination of ends. Economic conduct is not a thing apart from conduct in general. Moral, economic and other types of ends conflict and coincide with each other in precisely similar ways. Frequently the conflict of several different kinds of ends is involved in the same situation. A rational ordering of conduct is possible only on the basis that economic value is of like general character with other types of value.

5. Value theory of the traditional type, including utility and pain cost varieties, once possessed a functional and constructive validity. In the current situation, however, it no longer possesses that constructive validity.

6. Cultural reorganization involves the development of a new cultural mechanism as well as a new economic mechanism. It must involve also, eventually, the development of a new and different type of economic value theory.

108 THE DECADENCE OF VALUE THEORY

7. If the training for business administration is to afford leadership in a new profession, the newly created business school must take the lead in forecasting development of a new economic mechanism and a new system of value theory.[15]

[15] *Cf.* W. B. Donham, *op. cit.*

CHAPTER VI

THE BACKWARD OUTLOOK OF SOCIALISM

The socialist movement is a symptom and a result rather than a cause or instrument of social change. In so far as it is a factor in economic development, it belongs among the so-called negative factors discussed in Chapter IV.

Socialist and near-socialist writers have been permitted so to monopolize discussions of the disintegration of the competitive system that it behooves others who attempt anything of the sort to explain that they are not socialists and why they are not. If socialism isn't a substitute for competition why isn't it?

An answer to this question will not require a detailed appraisal of the merits and demerits of the socialist movement. It will not even be necessary to distinguish between different branches of the movement. All those groups which associate themselves more or less closely with the name of Karl Marx, the members of which argue from assumptions of social evolution and emphasize their opposition to institutions rather than individuals, are here taken together as a more or less homogeneous group. Stating the aims of this combined group in a rather vague, idealistic fashion, it seeks a more or less revolutionary reorganization of economic and social institutions. Man, so the argument runs, once was largely at the mercy of his physical environment. He dwelt in caves fashioned by natural forces unguided by human direction. But modern man fashions a dwelling for himself and equips it for a life of convenience and comfort undreamed of by the savage cave dweller. And this modern dwelling is only typical of the many ways in which the modern man has acquired mastery over the resources of his physical environment.

The social structure in which men live is, after all, only a larger, more intangible sort of dwelling. It has been a structure fashioned by unguided natural processes. The socialist wishes to do for it what man already has done for his physical habitation in substituting the modern dwelling for a cave. The socialist seeks to extend man's control of his physical environment so that it shall include his social environment as well. Man, he argues, after being for so long the victim of an unguided economic system, is to take the helm and give coherence and co-ordination to efforts which heretofore so frequently have run to cross purposes—thereby nullifying each other. The accuracy and economy of science, it is argued, is to supplant at once the wastefulness of natural processes and the exploitation incident to a conscious control of industry by a particular class in its own interests.

Such, in very broad outline, is the socialist ideal. Of course no moderate socialist expects a sudden detailed making over of society. He is content with making a beginning by group control of large scale productive operations. Notwithstanding some efforts even among present day socialists to describe characteristics and institutions of the socialist state, they mostly refrain from such description and insist that what is attempted along that line is highly tentative. This absence of an agreed-upon scheme of socialist institutions is not significant one way or another except as an indication of sanity and moderation upon the part of those socialist leaders who insist upon its necessity. The movement is not to be judged thereby.

THE PHILOSOPHY OF SOCIALISM

Going back to our own fundamental assumption with regard to the development of any particular scheme of institutions, we are led to ask, not what particular institutional forms do socialists advocate, but what is the philosophy of socialism.

The philosophy of socialism is to be culled from its stated ends, its arguments and its programs of reform. To Marx socialism was to be a working-class movement. Its excuse for existence was to be the overthrow of exploiting economic authority and a restoration of his rights to the worker. The chief right so to be restored was the right of the worker to "the whole product of his labor."

Coming down to a present-day spokesman for socialism, we have from Ramsay MacDonald the following: "So far from abolishing property, it (socialism) desires to establish it upon the only basis which makes property secure, that of service—of creative service."[1]

Both Marx and MacDonald claim that socialism holds

[1] *Socialism* (selections), p. 103.

out to labor the hope of reward in proportion to creative service. Underlying the statements of both are the assumptions of an individualistic viewpoint which also underlie the competitive system.

Turning to another point of socialist theory, we find that the doctrine of equality is held almost universally in some form or other. The notion of a classless state is a reincarnation of the idea that all men are created free and equal. The doctrine of equality may appear at one time as an "approximate equality of property," or again as "equality of opportunity," or it may be merely the democracy of a Kautsky; but, whatever its form, it is another expression of the philosophy of that same individualistic, democratic cultural period.

Socialist writers themselves have insisted upon the point that there is no antithesis between socialism and individualism. They might go even further and insist that socialist philosophy is individualistic. The platform of the socialist party of the United States for the campaign of 1904 asserted that the socialist party was "the only political movement standing for the program and principles by which the liberty of the individual may become a fact." And further, "it comes to rescue the people from the fast-increasing and successful assault of capitalism upon the liberty of the individual."

The socialist protest is essentially a criticism of the results of market control and is based fundamentally upon the philosophy underlying the theory of market control. This fact, no doubt, in part explains why the working classes have not been more apt in recognizing and giving adherence to a party ready made for them. It also affords a sidelight upon the circumstance that those who are ardent socialists so frequently are persons with a highly individualistic outlook.

The more positive formulations of socialists present the philosophical point of view here attributed to the movement even more strongly than the foregoing citations. Establishment of the socialist state following upon a period of education is to be a conscious assumption of responsibility. "Socialism, rightly understood, is the control of economics by associated men who have attained to the requisite insight and capacity." [2]

Discussions of the organization of a socialist state, such as the above quotation, afford a perfect example of the social contract theory. Socialism proposes to eliminate economic injustice and reestablish economic freedom of individuals by a social contract method of reorganization.

It is not to be denied that evolutionary socialists frequently take an objective point of view in their historical analysis of the development of institutions. But this philosophical viewpoint does not furnish the aims of the movement or afford the movement its excuse for existence. There is a hiatus between the socialist's objective historical study and his subjectively guided propaganda. He is seeking to make over prevailing institutions in such a fashion as to bring them into harmony with both a

[2] Kirkup, *A Primer of Socialism*, p. 85.

present technology and a philosophical viewpoint which was associated with an earlier scheme of technological processes. He is attempting to recast prevailing institutions without a new philosophical basis for the process. In the language of the shop, he is trying to rework his material without a new application of heat.

One of the figures of speech often used by socialist propagandists presents the current economic system as a much-patched garment which eventually has reached the time when it must be replaced new. The process of patching, it is argued, cannot go on forever. But when social evolution is viewed a little more broadly than socialists view it, their argument recoils upon themselves. Their program appears as merely just a little more comprehensive sort of patchwork. Paradoxical as the statement appears on its face to be, the socialist movement is, in its philosophical bearings, altogether reactionary.[8] Its position as a movement of protest alone saves it from being reactionary in practical effect as well as in philosophical outlook.

For further illustration, quoting again from MacDonald, "the state where life alone will be valued as treasure and the tyranny of the economic machine will no longer hold spiritual things in subjection. That state I call Socialism."

He wishes to preserve the economic machine and free spiritual things from its tyranny without providing a

[8] *Cf.* Davenport, *Economics of Enterprise—Introduction.* Professor Davenport pointed out the reactionary character of the socialist's economic theory.

spiritual regeneration. His dogma recognizes an evolution of economic methods but it fails to appreciate the evolution of philosophical viewpoints.

The shortcoming of the socialist movement here criticised is recognized by Rudolph Eucken who calls it a "spiritual sterility." Eucken's viewpoint does not agree with the one assumed in this discussion, but he does effectively call attention to the philosophical emptiness of the socialist movement. He writes, "Above and beyond all particular questions and tasks is the problem of man as a whole. It can only be approached with prospect of success if we take it in its historical connection and bring about a real revolution. We need new possibilities; a new attitude of men towards reality." [4]

The implications of this statement are, first, that socialists do not propose a real revolution, and second, that a real revolution would be a new attitude of men towards reality, that is, a new philosophical outlook. And he is right on both counts. The socialist program is not a constructively revolutionary program. The socialist state, so-called, is not a prophecy of the future but a ghost conjured up from the past.

SUMMARY

1. The socialist's ideal is a making over of man's cultural environment in a fashion comparable to the way in which he has developed his physical habitation.

2. The socialist's proposed method is a revolution by agreement—a social contract.

[4] *Socialism; An Analysis*, p. 111.

3. But socialist philosophy is the same as that which underlies the competitive régime. Socialism cannot lead to a cultural reorganization because a new philosophy is necessary for the shaping and fusion of a new system of institutions.

CHAPTER VII

THE SCIENTIFIC POINT OF VIEW

Socialism does not stand for constructive cultural development. But where shall we find that essential basis of social reconstruction which socialism lacks? A possible answer to this query is to be found in the modern scientific point of view.

There is a sophomoric attitude towards modern science which looks upon it as the fountain of truth. Devotees of such a view conceive that after thrashing around in the dark for countless generations, following one will-o'-the-wisp after another, believing first in this ism and then in that one, man finally has hit upon the truth in modern science. Scientists, working in the seclusion of their laboratories, are pictured as wresting from nature her immutable, everlasting laws.

Is this a fair picture?

What is science?

Experts will say that there is no such thing as general science; that all that is scientific will be found to belong in one or another of numerous special fields of investigation. And so true is this that almost anyone with a little ingenuity and some spare time can set up his private field of investigation and have a science all his own.

But back of all such special fields of investigation is a philosophy which gives unity to them all. When we speak of the modern scientific movement, we refer, not to the advancement of knowledge in particular fields of investigation, but to the spread of a philosophical point of view which underlies all of them.

The scientific point of view is among us today the court of highest appeal. Courts of law resort to it; legislatures defer to it; religious teachers borrow from it, and all classes acknowledge its authority. It is the one unifying influence which affords reasonable prospect of a general agreement. In case of any conflict of jurisdictions its voice prevails. It is more powerful, though less spectacular, than race prejudice, patriotism or religious conviction. Even those who attack it are careful to provide for a "proper scientific point of view." Even those who deny the adequacy of its philosophy recognize its cultural significance.[1] It is in fact the dominant factor in our present culture and other factors of necessity adjust themselves to it.

Nevertheless, the modern scientific movement is only a habit of describing the world of experience directly or indirectly in the objective terms of sense impression. There is nothing absolute or final about it. Indeed the conclusion to be drawn from its employment is that in time its dominance will be superseded by the dominance of other habits. But even this last qualification does not detract in the least from its present significance.[2]

[1] For example, "that there is a real world, which our senses more or less truly perceive, . . . is one of the presuppositions of our age." Royce, *The Spirit of Modern Philosophy*, p. 312.

[2] Science is today a fetish. As a result many strange points of view seek to attach to themselves the scientific appellation. The argument of each seems to be that it is most fundamental and

The relation between a spread of the philosophy of science and advancement of scientific work in the different fields of investigation is apt to be a matter of some dispute. Is the spread of the underlying viewpoint a by-product of advancement in the different fields or does it furnish the impetus behind such investigations? Doubtless it may be useful to say that the causal relation runs both ways. The possibility of argument as to which way it does actually run arises from an abstraction of the two concepts from the process which they both represent. When that process is viewed as a whole the scientific movement appears as a general cultural trend. When the movement is so interpreted the genius in scientific work maintains his relative position but loses some of the halo about his head. His glory is somewhat dimmed by the view that the advancement of science is after all a matter of objective cultural development. If our thinking about scientific matters is always carefully objective, questions of honorific distinction and priority of formulation are of small consequence.

therefore most truly scientific. Thereby homage is paid to the point of view which has made science a fetish.

The term science owes its prestige to the efforts of men to explain things not understood before in terms of sense experience. The viewpoint involved in that effort is entirely objective. Whether or not the objective viewpoint has exclusive right to the term science is after all merely a matter of terminology. Perhaps the term science should be abandoned altogether.

SCIENTIFIC METHOD

The habit of explaining experience by means of systematic formulations in objective terms obtained its dominant standing first in the physical sciences. So great has been its priority there that workers in the physical sciences sometimes regard themselves as the only scientists. Biologists are accepted as at least pseudo-scientific but social scientists so-called frequently are not admitted even to the antechamber of the scientific fraternity hall.

What, precisely, is the basis of this discriminating attitude? It of course does not rest upon any assumption of greater importance or greater ability on the part of the physical scientist. He is no more given to vanity in such matters than are other men. His claim rests rather upon his more consistent adherence to the objective point of view and upon the greater dependability of his conclusions; his ability to predict and the possibility of other men checking his conclusions. Other men can repeat his experiments and get the same results. Thus a maximum of cooperation is possible. A theoretical structure is built up and becomes the abstract presentation of a physical science.

By such cooperative efforts man's understanding of the physical and chemical aspects of his environment has been immensely increased and his power over his physical environment correspondingly extended. The magnitude of results so obtained in the physical sciences has given rise to the current prestige of the scientific point of view.

Progress of the objective viewpoint in those fields which

have been mapped out as the biological sciences has been slower than in the physical sciences, in part because of the greater complexity involved.[3] Experimentation is freely possible in biological subjects but upon a somewhat different plan. An agricultural experiment station, for example, is a much more unwieldy instrument than a physics or chemistry laboratory. Indeed the complexity of biological phenomena might well have successfully resisted inclinations of men to explain them in objective terms but for the prestige which the objective viewpoint had acquired earlier in the physical sciences. Successful application of the objective viewpoint in explanation of some parts of their experience has exerted a powerful pressure upon men to apply the same method to other portions of their experience. Speaking in figurative language, it is this momentum of the habit of thinking in objective terms which makes the scientific movement the dominant cultural trend of the current period.

Men working in the biological field under the influence of this movement have encountered the difficulty of the complexity of phenomena involved. They have in part at least overcome the difficulty. Out of the struggle of their efforts against the resistance encountered have come

[3] A distinction is sometimes drawn between physical and biological sciences by which physical science is presented as dealing in static terms or with homogeneous units whereas biology is said to be concerned with variation and change. This distinction is superficial. It overlooks the fact that geology and certain aspects of astronomy characteristically run in terms of evolution and change. At the same time it ignores the tendency of biology to explain variation in mechanistic or constant terms.

new methods for the application of the objective viewpoint. The methods of biological science do not in every respect follow those of physical science. And of chief importance among the biologist's contribution to methods is his development of the use of statistics. He did not originate the statistical method but it has proved a useful tool for his purposes and by using it successfully he has prepared the way for its use in other fields also. In the meantime, it has greatly furthered an application of the objective viewpoint to biological phenomena.

The statistical method is in its fundamental function the same as the method of rigid isolation of causes used in physical science laboratories. It, too, is a means of establishing or discovering causal or uniform relationships. It is applicable to complex phenomena to which the other method does not apply. One eliminates causes of variation by a rigid determination of experimental conditions. The other eliminates causes of variation by the inclusion and joint consideration of a large number of instances. Neither is automatically infallible. Both afford dependable results.

The term scientific method covers all the ways in which an objective viewpoint is applied to man's experience. In practice the term is made to cover more than this, but such extensions tend to take away its significance. Scientific method, as here used, is the manner in which the habit of objective thinking spreads. To illustrate by analogy, one would hardly speak of the method but rather the manner in which a forest fire spreads. And when one accepts the viewpoint assumed for this discussion, the scientific movement, viewed as a cultural trend, must be considered as free of supernatural direction as is the forest fire and like it causally determined.[4] And just as the manner in which a forest fire spreads varies with different conditions in different parts of the forest, so the manner in which the scientific movement spreads varies with the varying subject matters of the different sciences. There is no reason to suppose that the scientific movement may not, as it proceeds, give rise to still other methods. Indeed it is developing new technique in the social sciences. Investigation in the social sciences may very well lead to new methods which are as distinct as the isolated laboratory experiment and the statistical method.

An objective presentation of the scientific movement as a whole is valuable as a means of appraising its cultural significance. However, an attempt to use objective forms of expression without terms that are truly objective, or without truly objective assumptions, is apt to lead to the smothering and effective concealment of those relations which it is our intention to elucidate. If we hold that some social phenomena are subject to explanation in terms of cause and effect, but not all of them, we forsake the objective viewpoint which has been the basis of modern science. And if we still attempt to employ objective forms of expression the result is a deplorable confusion.[5]

---

[4] Of course causally determined means merely that it is explainable, or is assumed to be explainable, in objective, mechanistic terms of sense experience.

[5] *Cf.* Boucke, *A Critique of Economics, Doctrinal and Methodological.* A horrible example.

THE OBJECTIVE VIEWPOINT AND SOCIAL PHENOMENA

Discussion of the scientific movement in relation to social phenomena involves two distinct questions. The first of these is the formulation in objective terms of principles explaining social phenomena. It constitutes the social sciences. The second is the effect of a prevalence of objective habits of thought upon social phenomena, that is, the influence of such a philosophical viewpoint in the shaping of cultural organization.

In the formulation of the social sciences much already has been done—particularly in the application of the statistical method to problems in the fields of economics and sociology. But in comparison with what remains to be done not much has been accomplished. If one weighs the difficulties still to be met, in contrast with one individual's limited capacity, the task appears hopeless. But if one remembers that scientific accomplishment is a cooperative product, that it is, after all, a matter of cultural development, the situation takes on a quite different aspect. The small degree of cooperative accomplishment in the past and the present lack of theoretical structures running purely in objective terms, merely show that social sciences are in the early stages of their development.[6]

However, the scientific viewpoint is one whatever the subject matter to which it is applied. There is no supe-

[6] For comparison of the development of methods in economics with the development of methods in physical sciences, *Cf.* "Quantitative Analysis and the Evolution of Economic Science," by J. C. Cobb in *The American Economic Review*, Vol. 16, p. 426.

riority or essential difference in the philosophy applied in one field as against that applied elsewhere. Physical, biological and social sciences are all parts of one philosophical and cultural development.

The bearing of objective habits of thought upon social phenomena already has been suggested in the presentation of the scientific movement as the dominant influence in our own culture. Referring to the place of science in the current social organization, a recent economist has written as follows:

"The cultural structure clusters about this body of matter of fact knowledge as its substantial core. Whatever is not consonant with these opaque creations of science is an obtrusive feature in the modern scheme, borrowed or standing over from the barbarian past." [7]

The above statement may perhaps err in giving the impression that the percentage of cultural material "borrowed, or standing over from the barbarian past" is relatively small. Surely it is not. It would be more accurate to present the cultural clustering about the scientific point of view as a process now under way rather than as an "accomplished fact."

TECHNOLOGY AND THE SCIENTIFIC VIEWPOINT

Professor Veblen wrote further as follows:

"In modern culture, industry, industrial processes and industrial products have progressively gained upon humanity, until these creations of man's ingenuity have latterly come to take the dominant place in the cultural

[7] Veblen, *The Place of Science in Modern Civilization*, p. 2.

scheme; and it is not too much to say that they have become the chief force in shaping men's daily life, and therefore the chief factor in shaping men's habits of thought. Hence men have learned to think in the terms in which the technological processes act.... And so long as the machine process continues to hold its dominant place as a disciplinary factor in modern culture, so long must the spiritual and intellectual life of this cultural era maintain the character which the machine process gives it." [8]

This and other passages of Veblen's writings clearly imply a technological determination of the current scientific point of view. For explanation of machine technology he offered the unanalyzed process of cumulative change and the fortuitous circumstance that Great Britain is an island.[9] He of course admitted and insisted upon an interaction between the two. For example, "In both, the terms of standardization, validity, and finality are always terms of impersonal sequence, not terms of human nature or of preternatural agencies. Hence the easy co-partnership between the two. Science and technology play into one another's hands." [10]

But in spite of this stated assumption of interaction there clearly runs through his discussions an imputation of priority to technology.

Perhaps just as good a case and possibly a better one

[8] *The Place of Science in Modern Civilization,* p. 17.
[9] *Theory of Business Enterprise,* pp. 304-5.
[10] *The Place of Science in Modern Civilization,* p. 17.

TECHNOLOGY AND SCIENCE

could be made out for priority of the scientific viewpoint. Appreciable beginnings of modern scientific knowledge preceded the development of machine technology. Furthermore, the widely divergent and geographically scattered parts of the machine process, viewed in its widest sense, show an essential coherence which necessitates an analysis of the cumulative process by which they have come about. Such an analysis leads directly to the matter-of-fact, scientific knowledge underlying machine technology.

But there is no need to argue over the priority of science as against technology, or the reverse. Both may best be interpreted as phases of one process; as aspects of one cultural development. Our habit of dividing our activities into the two processes of discovering truth and then applying it, or of applying it and then discovering it, rests upon abstractions from the actual process. It is true after a fashion to say that man's knowledge of the physical sciences has enabled him to produce a much larger volume of economic goods. However, another description of precisely the same phenomena would be to say that man has been so controlled by his experience summed up in certain abstract principles that a much larger volume of economic products has resulted. Man's much vaunted control over nature can be expressed more aptly by putting man inside the process and describing the situation in terms of control over his actions. Man is in fact controlled by his knowledge of scientific principles. He is not outside the sphere of causal determination. By recognition of this fact and insistence upon it at all times, development of the social sciences will take place.

The necessity of keeping man within the social process has been made a basis for distinguishing the social sciences from the physical sciences.[11] Such a view assumes that the physical scientist does somehow get himself outside of the scheme of physical processes which he studies. It appears to involve a hidden assumption of dualism.

If one adopts the viewpoint of a mechanistic monism, he must recognize that his point of observation and his observation itself are both within the mechanism. But the physical scientist is no more free from this limitation than is the social scientist.

Whether work in the social sciences should take the assumption of a mechanistic monism as its most fundamental foundation, is a question which well may be argued on its own merits. Also it well may be questioned whether it is desirable to apply the same term, that is the term science, to different types of work which are done on the basis of different fundamental assumptions. Of course no student should be disposed to quarrel for possession of a particular label, however much prized it may be. The only important consideration is a common understanding in the use of terms.

When Professor Young, in the above citation, draws a line of fundamental distinction between the relation of the physical scientist to physical phenomena and the rela-

[11] *Cf.* A. A. Young, "Economics as a Field of Research," *Quarterly Journal of Economics*, Vol. 42, p. 2.

tion of the social scientist to social phenomena, the distinction appears to rest upon Professor Young's own assumption as to the nature of social phenomena. He appears to have been unwilling to extend the physical scientist's assumption of mechanistic monism to social phenomena. If one is willing to make this extension the distinction disappears.

That Professor Young did not accept a fundamentally mechanistic theory of society is indicated by his treatment of the contractual and mechanistic views of society as identical. It appears again in his statement that "history is true in the way that a picture is true." His position that social phenomena are not generally or fundamentally mechanistic in character is expressed in the phrase that they "may be in some measure determinate" in the narrow field of a particular social science. Mechanism is thus presented as a subordinate concept in the social sciences.

In the writer's view the mechanistic assumption should be fundamental and any necessary use of assumptions or methods not in harmony with it should be subordinate. Of course the social sciences are to be differentiated from the physical sciences by differences in subject matter. The practical difficulties confronting the social scientist are much greater. But if he starts from the assumption of a mechanistic monism, the social scientist's philosophical difficulties are precisely the same as those of the physical scientist who starts with the same assumption.

It is in his failure to keep the individual inside society

that the socialistic propagandist goes astray. The socialist is correct in his insistence that intelligent control will play a larger part in the social and economic affairs of the future than it has played in those of the past. The conduct of men in the future will be more controlled than it has been in the past by appreciation and understanding of causal relations obtaining between social phenomena. Man's inevitable future control over his social environment will be of precisely the same character as his alleged control over his physical environment. It will consist of a control over his conduct by abstract principles relating to social phenomena.

The development of social institutions determined by an understanding of social science is forcefully suggested by Dean Roscoe Pound's language in a discussion of the necessity for a revision of legal fundamentals. He writes as follows:

"The futility of a self-sufficing, self-centered science of law has become apparent to jurists. In politics and in sociology the results of centuries of judicial experience deserve to be regarded more than they have been in the past. But far more in jurisprudence the results of present day social surveys and the knowledge gained by the activities of the army of social workers that have taken upon themselves to do what among other peoples would be left to the state, must be put in the very forefront of that science. Its main problem today is to enable and to compel lawmaking and also the interpretation and application of legal rules to take more account and more intelligent account of the social facts upon which law must proceed and to which it must be applied.[12]

In short, the law must be made to agree with those principles which explain the social facts. The law which is to guide the conduct of men is thus to be shaped by precisely the sort of abstract principles above mentioned.

Persons steeped in the habit of thinking in subjective terms sometimes get the notion that development of an ability to predict in social affairs would free social phenomena from causal determination by making such phenomena subject to human control. They appear to think of social phenomena as retaining their present characteristics, that is, as remaining constant, while man learns to control them. They thereby put man outside of society. They do not seem to appreciate that an understanding of social phenomena running in objective terms would, if it became general, constitute or involve a fundamental change of social phenomena. Such an illusion is corrected by including man in the causal process.

Development of man's ability to predict in social affairs, a change which commonly is thought of in subjective terms as a conscious control of such phenomena, will merely constitute a more complex form of social organization. The difference between civilized man and the primitive savage is essentially in the relative complexity of their relations to their environments. The primitive man's life was simple. The causal complex bearing upon

[12] "Social Problems and the Courts," *American Journal of Sociology*, Vol. 18, p. 341.

each one of his actions was relatively simple. As man has become more civilized the causal complexes bearing upon his conduct have become more and more complex. At the same time the resultants of those causal complexes have become correspondingly more varied in the form of more varied lines of action. In this sense and in this sense only the individual has become more free. He has become a more complex mechanism for the transformation of causes into conduct. This development of the individual is still in process. It is quite conceivable that a thoroughgoing application of the objective viewpoint to social phenomena may be the means of making the individual of some future period as different from the civilized man of today as the latter is different from the most primitive form of human life.

FUTURE OF THE SCIENTIFIC VIEWPOINT

The fact that science and machine technology are aspects of one process of cultural development does not in any way insure their joint continuance. In one of the above quotations, Professor Veblen wrote that "so long as the machine process continues to hold its dominant place as a disciplinary factor in modern culture, so long must the spiritual and intellectual life of this cultural era maintain the character which the machine process gives it." This statement is open to the interpretation that so long as the machine process remains the dominant feature of economic production, the accompanying spiritual and intellectual life must retain its scientific bias. Behind the statement appears to lie the assumption that the economic factor always dominates cultural development. And that assumption, to say the least, is open to question.

If we accept the argument that a new social adjustment is being worked out under the dominant influence of the scientific point of view, what may we expect to follow that adjustment? Perhaps Professor Veblen would have said that by that time the process of cumulative change will so have altered the current system of technology that a new adjustment will be required. Such an answer would be in harmony with the assumption of a continued cultural dominance by the factor of technology and a more or less continuous conflict between institutions and their economic environment. However, the assumption of a continuous process of cumulative technological change is gratuitous. The rapid technological advance of the last 150 years has been the development of a definite system of technology rather than a mere section from an undifferentiated and unending process of technological evolution. Indeed technology is itself a cultural matter rather than an outside or environmental factor bearing upon culture. Economic development and technological development, as well as development of the individual, must be provided for within the process of cultural change.

Western culture of the modern period has been dominated, to date, by economic interests. Economic development has attracted a lion's share of man's capacities and efforts because it offered the obvious and apparently the largest task to be performed. The logic of the situation in which man has found himself in this period has directed human efforts in that direction. Without doubt other interests have languished. But these facts afford neither proof nor presumption that a similar cultural emphasis will continue. If anything, they, taken in conjunction with other facts, are evidence of a turning point to come; a turning point leading away from the economic interest. As the writer reads the trend of cultural evolution the present overwhelming pressure for standardization, which is incident to the machine process, precludes an even continuance of the past rapid development of technology. It points rather to the coming of a relatively static period in the process of technological evolution; a period which by comparison bids fair to reduce the traditional static organization of the Middle Ages to a diminutive embryo. The machine process in its fully developed state appears destined to furnish the basis for such a period of economic stability.[18] If this reading is correct and the scientific point of view shapes the development of a cultural organization in consonance with such an economic foundation, there is no reason apparent why the intellectual capacities of men should stagnate because of economic stability. The "spiritual and intellectual" interests of men would then be free to seek new pastures green.

There seems to be some basis for a conclusion that the next major move of cultural evolution, some hundreds of years hence, will not be in the field of economic development and will not be determined by the economic factor

[18] *Cf.* footnote to p. 169.

SUMMARY

of culture.[14] In speaking of a next move, we assume that the present major development is a readjustment of cultural organization under the influence of the scientific point of view.

SUMMARY

1. The advancement of science is a cultural movement based upon the spread of a philosophical point of view; a habit of thinking in objective terms.

2. The scientific movement and the development of machine technology are two aspects of one cultural development. Together they constitute the dominant trend of this cultural period.

3. This dominant influence is shaping a social readjustment which may be counted upon to result in a re-unified social organization.

4. Man's alleged control over his physical environment is better expressed by including man in the process and expressing the situation as a control over man's actions by his experience summed up in abstract principles. In the same way man's social environment of the future will be determined by his actions which will be increasingly controlled by abstract formulations summing up his social experience.

5. A fuller understanding of social phenomena will not relieve man from being subject to a causal deter-

---

[14] Hobson, *Evolution of Modern Capitalism*, p. 365. Also, Seligman, *Economic Interpretation of History*, p. 155. Both Hobson and Seligman suggest such a cultural shift away from economic interests.

mination of his actions. It will mean merely that still more complex social adjustments are possible; the development of a more complex individual and a more complex society.

6. The standardization which is a characteristic feature of the machine process, and of the civilization which is developing therewith, points to a relatively static period of maximum economic and social stability.

7. With economic stability on a large scale covering a long period, some cultural factor or factors other than the economic may be counted upon to assume the dominant rôle. Hence such a cultural shift appears imminent —that is, it appears likely to come some hundreds of years hence.

CHAPTER VIII

DEVELOPMENT OF MODERN BUSINESS MANAGEMENT

Trading for profit is not peculiar to the modern period in which, among Western peoples, economic interests have predominated over all other interests. Nevertheless the conditions of modern economic life have caused business enterprise, or trading for profit, to undergo a change which has made it distinct from earlier forms of such enterprise.

The extent of modern division of labor has meant a practically universal production for market. This emphasis upon business enterprise has been accompanied by a development of large scale activity which has brought with it the evolution of new machinery of business control. These changes have altered essentially the problems of business administration.

BUSINESS MANAGEMENT AND TECHNOLOGY

Large scale enterprises were known prior to the industrial revolution. They were then confined principally to the field of commerce or trade. Historical observation however discloses, in general, a trend from smaller to larger units of enterprise during the dominance of the competitive system. It is characteristic of both European and American experience but is particularly pronounced in the United States. The industrial revolution stimulated but did not initiate the development here cited.

This general trend has not been equally characteristic of all lines of business enterprise nor has it been regular and continuous in any of them. Nevertheless it has been a general tendency.

The development from smaller units to larger units has included both business and technological aspects. Upon the business side, the development runs from the single trader to the partnership, to the joint stock company, to the limited liability corporation, to various forms of super-corporate organization. On its technological side the unit of enterprise shows a somewhat similar line of development. Under even the craft organization of handicraft industry a tendency is to be observed towards production by master workmen operating with an increasing number of employees. Later there follow in order, the organization of groups of handicraftsmen working for one employer under conditions approximating modern capitalistic production; the factory using natural power and based upon a high degree of division of labor; multiple factories with numerous interrelated processes, products and by-products, and finally the integration of a number of different industries.[1]

The first, or business phase of this development towards larger units, has to do with the management and control of the competitive unit and with the form of its appearance in the market. The latter phase has to do with the technological processes of production. Causes

[1] This description is intended to apply to characteristic developments in Great Britain and the United States.

which have contributed to the development of large scale operations have not been confined solely to either aspect of the process. Problems of finance, the mere assembling of requisite amounts of capital; centralization and continuity of control; financial strength under adverse business conditions, and the like, have all played important rôles in the process. Likewise the economy of effort and materials incident to quantity production, and other technological savings arising from the coordination of processes on a large scale, as well as also the possibility of producing thereby goods which could not otherwise be produced, have all been no less influential than have the business advantages of operations upon a large scale.

In this twofold classification of factors those connected with the ownership and control of the means and processes of production, and with the sale of products therefrom, are dubbed business considerations. Thereby they are distinguished from considerations relating to technical equipment and processes, the material and human equipment and technical knowledge with which business enterprise must operate and by which it is limited.

The development of particular units of large scale production has, of course, not always been influenced to the same degree by the two sets of factors. Some large enterprises have arisen more largely by reason of business arrangements; others from technological advantages, and still others from a more balanced operation of the two sets of causes. There would be no point in arguing that either set of causes is more or less natural or more or less artificial than the other. By stressing technological factors and making the increase of technological effectiveness synonymous with welfare one might be led to discount the importance of business factors. Socialists, for example, look with hostility upon any control of important technological processes by an overhead business organization. They appear sometimes to forget the necessity for some sort of overhead machinery of control.

On the other hand, by stressing business considerations, especially the historical fact that modern economic development has taken place under the control and direction of competitive business enterprise, one might easily be led to question the priority of technological efficiency over business organization. One might well conclude that the most important feature of any practical policy would be to preserve that incentive to private gain which has stimulated so much economic progress in the past. But any inquiry which claims to be scientific must look upon both business and technological factors with an entirely dispassionate attitude.

The modern period in which economic interests have held dominance over other human interests in North European countries, and latterly in the United States, must be dated from the rise of Italian cities to commercial importance.[2] The successful commercial enterprise there developed stands on the threshold of an economic expansion which stimulated and went hand in hand with geographic expansion. Peoples of northern Europe envied Italy her success; borrowed freely of her commercial

[2] This does not mean that there have not been other such periods in other cultures.

practices, and took commerce away from her as much and as quickly as possible. Italian commerce furnished a spirit of business enterprise. Handicraft technology furnished a discipline which stimulated the growth of habits of thought which made possible the development of a system of economic control through the free play of business enterprise. Under the joint influence of these two, the modern development of the market took its rise. Under the favorable circumstances inherent in an increasingly free market, business enterprise and a partly developed scientific point of view combined to produce modern machine technology. But now that machine technology has become the dominant discipline afforded by man's economic environment, it, with the assistance of a more fully developed scientific viewpoint, has turned upon its chief progenitor, business enterprise, and, taking its turn as a controlling factor, is making over the character of business administration.

REACTION OF TECHNOLOGY UPON MANAGEMENT

Out of the relative stagnation of the Middle Ages trading developed first as a somewhat grudgingly permitted activity carried on by a particular class of individuals.[3] Development of the individualistic scheme of social organization wrote a new foundation under commercial enterprise. It socialized trading by making it directly and explicitly related to group welfare. Business enter-

[3] It will hardly be questioned that commerce of the Middle Ages was relatively stagnant as compared with its modern development or with commercial activities of the Greeks and Romans.

prise became the cornerstone of a new system. The privilege of trading became the right of all free members of the community. As we have seen in an earlier chapter the completion of this change was marked by the absorption of the law merchant into the common law. That process of absorption thus is an index of an important social development. It is one of the high points in the development of an individualistic social organization. The coming in of such a form of economic organization gave free scope to business enterprise and established it upon a firm foundation without in any essential way changing its character. It is only when business enterprise encounters large scale operations based upon the machine process that it undergoes important change.

In the early modern trading companies a hierarchy of officials exercising delegated authority had been developed. The organization was fairly effective for such companies. Later forms of business enterprise in the field of production took over this organization but not with entire success. As soon as an enterprise developed to the point of having a large volume of technical operations, it required both a business administration and a technical organization. In industrial enterprises the technical organization came to head up in a factory superintendent, a works manager or some other technical executive. With increasing use of machine technology on a large scale, a line of cleavage between the business and technological aspects of competitive units became more and more typical. An increasing magnitude of the required machinery of business control shared responsibility for this development with the growth of technological organization. Through a separate development of the two organizations business management became more or less detached from technological operations.

The current tendency of economic organization is to close up the rift between business management and technological processes. In the first place, accounting has been developed to furnish management with better means of control than have been available in the past. This, accounting has done through a development of internal accounts, that is, development of the use of accounts for control within the business enterprise. Before the industrial revolution, accounting was mainly a record of the external relations of one business unit with other business units, a record of relations determined in the market. But with the advent of large scale productive operations and the grouping of many interests within the competitive unit carrying on such operations, necessity arose for more emphasis upon the accounting for interests within the competitive unit and upon the use of accounting records as a means of administrative control over the enterprise. The introduction of centralized accounting departments, as for example in the railway business,[4] is an illustration of this development. The appearance of cost accounts in manufacturing, affording business management a more direct control over technological processes, is another example.

[4] *Cf.* Nay, "Uniform Methods of Railway Accounting," in *The Journal of Political Economy*, Vol. 21, p. 881.

A REVOLUTION IN MANAGEMENT

A second process tending to close the gap between business management and technological operations is a change which is coming over business management itself. This change has not developed as far as the improvement of accounting technique, and its effect cannot in the nature of the case be so immediate, yet it appears destined to be in the long run even more far-reaching and fundamental. The change here referred to results from the influence of machine technology upon the processes of business control and upon the point of view of management.

The effect of the machine process upon administrative control is closely associated with the development of accounts. It already has been noted that the development of large scale technical processes has necessitated a corresponding development of overhead machinery of control. Finance, sales, purchasing, accounting, general administration and other business departments require a large number of clerical employees in addition to various grades of executives. The duties of all of these administrative employees must be highly standardized and closely correlated in order that the departments to which they belong may function smoothly in relation to each other and in relation to the departments which are responsible for technological results. This highly organized force of employees becomes a means through which plans and policies of a central administration are carried out. Activities of all members of the force are standardized and reduced to routine as far as possible. The administrative organization has developed to the point of becoming machine-like. Starting mainly from the influence of a use of power-driven machines, standardization and the enforcement of a machine-like regularity have spread not only to all the processes of technological production but to the activities of the business administration as well.

The use of accounting forms and the building up of a systematic control over administrative operations have been the means of reducing such operations to routine. The use of a systematic accounting control has reacted upon both administrative and technical operations. Such a systematic control has been the means of bringing about a better coordination of human and mechanical elements in the productive process. Thereby it has made even particular technological processes more machine-like. Its more important contribution, however, has been in tying separate processes together in a larger machine-like unit. Not only have technical processes been tied more closely together, and administrative operations more closely coordinated, but at the same time the two groups of activities have been drawn into a single re-united organization. This fact is the basis for the statement that accounting has tended to bridge the gap between technological operations and business control.

The foregoing analysis has not reached beyond the mechanics of administrative control to the discretionary authority which directs the machinery of control. Such authority is itself undergoing a change of viewpoint under the influence of its changed environment.

In a market where the typical competitive interest was that of an individual, where enterprise was carried on in a comparatively small way, the problems of management were to a relatively large degree concerned with relations outside the enterprise. Problems of internal management and control were at a minimum both because of the manager's technical knowledge of the enterprise and on account of its relatively small size. Even the large trading companies which developed prior to the industrial revolution were comparatively simple in their internal organization and operation. In the case of the trading company and the small scale production unit, the unity of the enterprise was so obvious as to forestall any difficulty of thinking and planning in terms of the enterprise as a whole.[5]

The same cannot be said for a modern industrial enterprise. A unified view of a modern large scale enterprise is an exceedingly elusive thing obscured by a great variety of problems. The manager of such an enterprise is furnished a large mass of information upon many different phases of the business. And the information which he gets cannot be left to chance. It is quite as important for him to know what not to call for as it is to know how to use what he gets. External and internal considerations in

[5] The point here in question is not essentially a matter of size but of complexity. The multiplication of simple units does not create complexity. If it did we would have to concede complexity of the farmer's technology because he tends a very large number of hills of corn. Even the enterprises of the Fuggers did not constitute a complex system. Their technique of control did not include even a double entry system of bookkeeping.

A REVOLUTION IN MANAGEMENT

interminable variety must be weighed and balanced against each other. Neither the facts relative to cost of production nor those relating to markets to be served must be misread or ignored. Effective management requires a factual basis of information relative to all aspects of the enterprise. Without such information it cannot inaugurate successful policies. There is necessary also an intelligent, unbiased interpretation of the facts. Only in such a way can the manager succeed in thinking in terms of his business as a whole. Thus the biggest problem of all in modern management is one which was virtually no problem at all in the early history of modern business enterprises.

The collection and presentation of facts which management must use are dependent upon the use of comprehensive systems of accounting and statistical technique. Management, therefore, is becoming more and more dependent upon these indispensable tools. The persistent trend towards still larger operations, and the practical necessity for a close coordination between administration and the accomplishment of basic technological results, appear to guarantee continued development along the same line. Indeed mere competitive pressure for survival seems bound to force upon each particular management a more and more thoroughgoing use of accounting and statistical methods of control. And the effective use of such methods is dependent upon an intelligent and unbiased appraisal of many different pertinent factors. This means that the development of the machine process has reached a point at which it is tending to force upon the business manager habits of thought which are consistently objective.[6]

The discipline associated with the conduct of business enterprise, thus, has undergone, or at least is undergoing, a process of complete change. When the market was composed of individualistic interests, trading for a profit tended to enforce habits of thought in the subjective terms of individual self-interest. But the conditions of business management have so changed, under the influence of modern technology, that the predominating discipline involved in it is one which impels objective habits of thought. Thus the philosophy of management is being converted to that of the prevailing scientific point of view.

The foregoing statement does not mean that particular business men are being converted to a new point of view by a change in the conditions of their work. It is not even argued that any considerable change is to be observed in the attitudes of successive generations of business men, though some change of that character surely is to be noted. The argument here is concerned with a change of discipline whose influence upon institutional-

[6] Emphasis upon the influence of the machine process should not be carried to the point of making it the exclusive origin or cause of the new bent in business management. For example, development of the corporate form of enterprise is an important factor in the shaping of modern business enterprise. While the machine process undoubtedly is responsible in part for the corporation's dominant rôle in modern business, it would be a mistake to ascribe the vogue of the corporation altogether to technological influences. The corporation, of course, ante-dates the machine process by a wide margin.

ized habits of thought is a slow but patient and unhurried process. The precise point of contention is that the prevailing cultural movement, which is represented in two different aspects by machine technology and the scientific point of view, is tending to bring about such a change. And in so doing it is helping to iron out the current friction or lack of coordination between business administration and technological operations.

STATISTICAL METHODS IN MANAGEMENT

Business management already has developed to a considerable degree in the use of statistical methods. An accounting executive for a large enterprise recently was in conference with students from a school of business administration with a view to their employment by the company he represented. He remarked incidentally that the first shock men coming out of school would have would be to find that the accounting for a large enterprise includes so much more than they had studied under that subject; that it in practice includes much statistical material which can in no way be expressed in the mechanics of double entry bookkeeping.

This statement constituted a serious criticism of what that man considered the conventional method of teaching accounting. At the same time it afforded some indication of how far business managements have gone in the use of statistical methods.

RESPONSIBILITIES OF MANAGEMENTS

Large scale business enterprise has made influential executives stewards of the properties which they control. In the shift which has taken place in the typical position occupied by business executives, it is inevitable that at first the individualistic attitude of self-interest should continue to be dominant even in the new situation. It is therefore to be expected that "inside rings" and various kinds of "stock jobbing" should develop during the earlier history of corporate administration. It is also to be expected that the development of an attitude of responsible stewardship on the part of business executives should be viewed with a great deal of skepticism. But the fact of such responsibility, .coupled with the development of checks to prevent mismanagement, may be counted upon to develop an attitude of management which is quite different from that of an unadulterated economic self-interest. Responsibility to stockholders already is pretty well developed and responsibility to consumers and to the public interest seem likely to follow a similar line of development. Such a result is not to be predicted upon the basis of any change of heart or brotherly love or altruism of business executives but solely upon a basis of the disciplinary influences to which they as a class are subject.

The changed discipline under which business enterprise operates is clearly presented when corporate management is contrasted with management of the business of an individual entrepreneur. The interest which is to be protected and furthered by the individual entrepreneur is obvious. True, the basis of the lone entrepreneur's choice does not appear so simple when we consider that he must weigh his future as well as his present interests. However, the cultural circumstances which gave rise to a competitive system gave rise also to numerous rules of economic conduct calculated to offset the importunities of the present and so help the individual entrepreneur steer an even course between present and future ends. These rules, or principles, have to do chiefly with industry, thrift and business-like conservatism. They are the sort of thing for which Poor Richard was noted. The development of such standards of business conduct is to be considered as part of the development of economic machinery of control just as truly as the development of the market itself. Indeed they were part of the individualistic market system.

With the change from individualistic to corporate management it was inevitable that much of the attitude of managers should be carried over from the old situation to the new. The emphasis of the old situation upon individual self-interest led logically to mismanagement, that is, management in the interest of one or a few stockholders at the expense of the rest. Similarly the rules of conservatism and thrift of the earlier period were carried over into corporate management where their application sometimes has resulted in unintentional mismanagement. At other times it has been a cloak of fraud.[7]

[7] *Cf.* W. Z. Ripley, "From Main Street to Wall Street," in *Atlantic Monthly*, Jan., 1926.

A more extensive development of the corporate form of management is tending to give a new attitude to management and to develop new standards of business conduct. An attitude of responsibility to stockholders is tending to supplant an earlier viewpoint of individual self-interest. This change is being fostered not only through approval of it by business men but also through the development of accounting and auditing technique calculated to disclose and to prevent mismanagement.

Responsibility to stockholders means more than a mere current accountability for funds. The management of corporate enterprise involves the formulation and execution of policies which overreach the bounds of a static responsibility. Management is responsible to a continuous group of stockholders, the members of which change from time to time. Hence the management is faced with the responsibility for balancing the interests of present and future stockholders. In drawing a line between such conflicting interests, the management is not much helped by such rule of thumb principles of thrift and conservatism as those which were developed in the individualistic period. Corporate management requires and is slowly developing more exact rules of its own.[8]

An attitude of business men, approving conservative

[8] For a discussion of the development of an attitude of responsibility on the part of corporate managements see "The Sherman Act: Its Design and Its Effect," by M. W. Watkins in *The Quarterly Journal of Economics*, Nov., 1928.

standards of business conduct and condemning actions contrary thereto, showed itself early in accounting. It still persists there, as for example in the prevailing but unjustifiable rule to take inventories at cost or market whichever is the lower. Under the influence of individualistic enterprise a general policy of conservatism became a standard dogma of accounting. It has been carried over into corporate accounts. It still is defended by practitioners and teachers of accounting. However, irrational conservatism must give way before the demand of managers for efficiency. In accounts, as in management, the dogma of conservatism must make way for a dogma of accuracy. And incidentally, in this connection, it should be a function of academic instruction in accounts to point the way of such development rather than to accept prevailing practice as a guiding standard.[9]

[9] It is interesting to note how the author of the currently leading introductory accounting text has been influenced by the two dogmas of conservatism and accuracy. In closing his discussion of depreciation he writes as follows:
"Except for the transient, speculative stockholder, a fixed depreciation policy based on a conservatively accurate allowance is always for the best interest of the property and its owners." Kester, *Accounting Theory and Practice,* Vol. II, p. 298.
Why should we not be recklessly and unreservedly accurate? The impossibility of attaining absolute accuracy never justifies an intentional understatement of assets and overstatement of expenses. If we know that we are given to overvaluation, accuracy may demand the discounting of our estimates of asset values. But if we merely wish to make provision against unknown possible inaccuracies, the only correct principle upon which to proceed is to set up a specific reserve for that purpose.
A somewhat similar illustration of the influence of the two dogmas

SCHOOLS OF BUSINESS MANAGEMENT

No discussion of business management could well omit passing reference to the recent appearance of schools of business administration although they are a rather incidental, not to say superficial, factor in the case. They represent a phase in the process of a standardization of business practices. Without standardization of business practices and methods, a preliminary discipline peculiar to the uses of future business men would be impossible. And the effect of a general application of such a discipline will be to hasten still more the process of standardization.

Two further effects may be counted upon to follow the development and application of a preliminary theoretical training for business men. One of these is the development of a distinctly professional attitude and the other is a certain amount of predisposition towards that objective point of view which the administration of practical business affairs is coming to demand.

here referred to, is to be found in J. O. McKinsey's *Managerial Accounting*, Vol. I, p. 176. He writes as follows:

"The preparation of the balance sheet of a going concern so as to state all the assets at conservative but full and fair values requires, among other things, the following . . ."

And among the rules which follow this introduction, as a requirement for arriving at full and fair values, is the conventional lower of cost and market rule.

It is generally true of Professor McKinsey that so far as technique is concerned, he whole-heartedly adopts a functional point of view but at the same time he has not freed himself from rules of thumb which are associated with the formal conception of accounting technique.

SUMMARY

1. Business enterprise was at a very low ebb in Europe during the Middle Ages. Trading for a profit was held, by an agricultural people, to be anti-social.
2. With renewed commercial activity, trading for profit made slow headway in the face of prejudice against it. Even after it became a proper vocation for Christians it remained in the hands of a special class.
3. The development of an individualistic, competitive society placed business enterprise upon a secure foundation. In fact it made trading for profit the very cornerstone of a new economic organization.
4. The prevailing discipline of this individualistic system was one which enforced upon those who conducted business enterprise habits of thought in the subjective terms of self-interest.
5. However, the use of machine processes and the development of large scale enterprise based thereon have developed a new discipline which tends to enforce upon business managers habits of thought in impersonal, objective terms.
6. The current discipline to which managers are subject may be expected to enforce an attitude of responsibility both to stockholders and to the public interest.
7. The period of individualistic management gave rise to numerous unofficial rules or standards of business conduct. These rules carried over into corporate management frequently gave rise to mismanagement and even fraud. Corporate management is bound to develop

and is now developing new standards of practice suited to its own environment.

8. These changes which are coming about in the activities and outlook of those who are in charge of business enterprise are merely some of the results of a prevailing cultural discipline which is moulding the institutions of a new cultural period.

CHAPTER IX

THE PROCESS OF SOCIAL READJUSTMENT

The proposition that a new and distinct cultural period is now in process of development has been advanced repeatedly in the foregoing chapters. In Chapter VIII the argument was carried a step further to show how business enterprise, which has played so important a rôle in the competitive system, is slowly but surely being remade. If the present discussion were a general treatment of the cultural change above mentioned it would be in point here to continue the argument along the same line. A logical procedure would be to show next the working of the prevailing objective discipline upon other economic groups, such as the labor, agricultural and professional groups, and then to summarize the process of readjustment as a whole.

Much could be done through the carrying out of such a plan. With respect to the agricultural group, for example, such an analysis would concern itself first with conditions surrounding the development of the so-called scientific management of the individual farm unit and with the development of a broader organization of agricultural interests. With respect to labor the analysis would start from the work which already has been done showing why wage workers have lost the philosophical point of view which underlies a competitive organization of society.

158 PROCESS OF SOCIAL READJUSTMENT

However, this book is not a comprehensive discussion of even the current trend of cultural development. Its concern is with the cultural setting and significance of accounts. Its scope is, therefore, both broader and narrower than the current cultural trend but it does not include that trend as such.

The present chapter is a mere parenthesis inserted to point out the inappropriateness of a general discussion of the current cultural trend. At the same time, however, we shall here compromise with the temptation to introduce such a discussion to the extent of pointing out something of the manner in which the actual cultural development of the near future may be expected to take place. Also we shall yield to the temptation to point a moral to the extent of giving a bit of advice to social scientists.

That a cultural revolution is now under way probably will not be denied by anyone who is in the habit of applying an evolutionary viewpoint to social phenomena.[1] Doubtless all who accept such an evolutionary notion, except socialists of the more radical varieties, will also agree that among English-speaking peoples, at least, the revolution may be expected to work itself out without

[1] "Only wiser men with a broader vision; an entirely different and more comprehensive understanding of interrelationships; a much improved social discipline; social instincts and moral and political institutions shaped in an entirely different fashion, can overcome the frictions and difficulties occasioned by a highly developed technique."—Schmoller, *Grundriss der allgemeinen Volkswirtschaftslehre*, Vol. I, p. 231. The translation is the writer's.

Cf. also note 5, p. 169.

violence. It must come as a causally determined, predictable process rather than as a subjectively guided, social contract type of reorganization. If past experience may be depended upon, it will not result in a classless organization of society.

The new order must develop from the existing situation. This current situation is pluralistic in the sense that opposing economic and social groups hold to radically different beliefs and do not recognize a common allegiance to one fundamental authority. An essential contention in the present discussion is, however, that present opposing groups do share a common though unrecognized allegiance in their faith in the scientific or objective point of view. The process of working out a social adjustment upon the basis of this viewpoint must of necessity be long and slow. It can take place only through the conflict of opposing groups; through negotiation and adjustment of opposing claims. It is not an academic problem which admits of a solution which can be handed down and applied. Not from choice on anybody's part, but from the necessities of the case, it must follow the rule of law that an adjudication must be based upon a real and not an assumed conflict of interests.

Under these circumstances, the best that the social scientist can do is to hold fast to the point of view upon which an adjustment is to rest; to look further into the process of adjustment than do those who represent the opposing interests at stake, and, so far as is possible, provide the contestants with objectively stated principles to guide their conduct in a fashion comparable to the way in which man's so-called conquest of his physical environment has been controlled by the principles of the physical sciences.

SUMMARY

1. The future of our culture must come out of its present situation through a causally determined, predictable process.

2. Our present cultural situation is characterized by a conflict of loyalties and beliefs.

3. However, in spite of their important differences, most present opposing groups share an unrecognized common allegiance to the objective or scientific point of view.

4. A social readjustment can be counted upon to work itself out through a process of conflict and compromise until the claims of opposing groups are harmonized upon the basis of the common viewpoint.

5. The function óf the social scientist in the premises is to look further into the process than the members of the contending groups are able to do and to provide them with objectively stated principles to guide or control their actions in working out a new *modus vivendi*.

CHAPTER X
SOME ASPECTS OF STANDARDIZATION

Uniformity is a necessary basis of social organization. Standardization of the terms in which social intercourse runs has always magnified both the possibilities and the actual scope of cooperation within the social group. The standardization of sounds into speech and the reduction of symbols to written language aided incalculably in the interchange of ideas and in their transmission from one generation to another. The standardization of purchasing power in monetary media and the standardization of weights and measures greatly facilitated the interchange of economic goods. Standardization of time measurement increased the possibilities of social cooperation immeasurably. Examples could be multiplied indefinitely. Even in the field of economic production, where we hear so much nowadays about the standardization of products, processes and equipment, standardization is nothing new. From time immemorial methods of production have been standardized. Primitive peoples have followed highly standardized processes in the making of such varied products as boats, weapons, houses and pottery.

Turning to a somewhat different field, the development of esthetic principles, the formulation of legal rules, the evolution of ethical standards, and indeed the setting up of norms in all lines of human activity are matters of standardization. In fact the development of distinct cultures and distinct cultural periods is in a broad sense a process of standardization. The institutions which at any given time make up the cultural structure are standardized to the extent that they are shaped to fit in with the prevailing viewpoint which gives coherence and unity to that culture. This does not mean that the ideas and actions of all those whom the culture represents run according to a single pattern. Even when our own culture was at the height of its late individualistic period, there still was much thinking in other than individualistic terms. The period took its name and character from the viewpoint which then served as the basis of social organization because it was dominant. But the mere statement that it was dominant implies the presence of other viewpoints.

In an approach to reorganization such as our culture is now making, standardization necessarily plays an important rôle. This would be true in any other similar period. Standardization is in no way peculiar to our situation. The thing which is significant now is the basis upon which the current process of standardization is taking place.

SCIENTIFIC MANAGEMENT

Before considering the general significance of the current trend towards standardization, it will be well to discuss some aspects of the movement in the narrower field of economic organization.

In an earlier chapter it was pointed out that the point

of view of management is coming to be more and more objective and that the rift and friction between business control and industrial processes give promise of disappearing. However, such a renewal of economic unity as is thus promised will require more than a mere device of organization, or form of administration, on the one hand, and more than the mere development of a common point of view on the other hand. It can come only through a remaking of institutional forms in consonance with a new point of view.

Scientific management, as associated with the name of the late Frederick W. Taylor, is essentially an application of the objective point of view in the directive control of industry. It involves a high degree of standardization. Its central thesis is that the methods and procedures of both industrial production and business control should be determined by a process of objective, unbiased experimentation. Wherever Taylor was able to apply this principle, the results achieved proved its great significance. In fact the results were so startling that one well may ask why the Taylor system has not immediately revolutionized the administration of all industry.

The slow headway scientific management has made frequently is ascribed to the opposition of organized labor. The resistance of labor is attributed to ignorance and to prejudice aroused by the misuse by executives of devices such as those involved in scientific management. Mismanagement of the sort which is bound to antagonize labor has sometimes been stimulated by pseudo-management experts like one who characterized scientific management as "educating the employer and fooling the employees."

The foregoing explanation is essentially true as far as it goes. The factors mentioned are to be taken into account. But the explanation is too superficial to pass it without further analysis.

Taylor sought to eliminate waste effort and friction from industrial operations. Where, by his demonstrated ability and the force of his personality, he won the support of business executives and workers, there resulted a common adherence to his system which went far towards elimination of the perennial friction between employers and workers. If there were a Frederick W. Taylor in each enterprise of the country a general revolution of industrial and business management would, no doubt, soon be effected. The combined influence of such a number of such men would in all probability overcome even the resistance which is now offered to the use of Taylor methods. But such a result is far different from what actually has followed a general promulgation and particular applications of Taylor's ideas.

It is true that an essential obstacle to the development of objectively determined methods and standards of industrial and business control lies in the divergence of views of employers and workers. The viewpoint of employers is largely a more or less blind adherence to the principles underlying the open market. Labor, on the other hand, has lost faith in the machinery and even in the principle of market control. Hence, as long as scien-

SCIENTIFIC MANAGEMENT

tific management is a form of control associated with the competitive control of industry it must meet the hostility and suspicion of the labor group. It is quite conceivable that if competitive managements had always made intelligent use of the principles of scientific management, the faith of laborers in market control and their respect for the notions of property and property rights inherent in market control would never have been destroyed. But since that faith has been lost it is not to be restored by the proposal of scientific management or even by its successful application in particular cases.

Taylor, as a practical executive, made free use of coercive methods. Nevertheless, he sought, as a first principle, to bring about cooperation. Only in that way could an efficient industrial unit be achieved. He demanded agreement through acceptance of objectively determined methods and standards. He truly sought to bring a new spirit into industry. And that spirit is one of faith in the very objective point of view which we have presented repeatedly as the dominant cultural influence of the present time.[1] Hence we well may ask again why the Taylor system does not ride into universal use upon the crest of so powerful a movement even in spite of the opposition of labor!

It has been pointed out earlier that the socialist movement seeks to make over the institutional forms of economic organization without the service of a new phil-

[1] For an excellent and sympathetic interpretation of Taylor's life and work the reader is referred to Copley, *Frederick W. Taylor*. (Two volumes.)

osophical point of view to permit and to shape the development of new institutional forms. In contrast with the socialist position, Taylor and those of his disciples who have caught the spirit of his work seek to infuse a new spirit into the old processes of economic production and distribution.

Scientific management concerns itself with the immediate operation and administrative control of productive processes. It does not touch the problem of distribution. Its tacit acceptance of orthodox machinery for the determination of distributive shares involves it in a fundamental incongruity. An economic system resting upon productive processes dominated by the objective attitude of Taylor is an attractive ideal. But the ideal is only fragmentary. An economic system so constituted as to its productive processes but including at the same time a competitive system of distribution, with its proverbial subjective foundations, would indeed be a monstrosity. And yet that is the sort of organization which scientific management has to offer. With regard to distribution, Taylor himself did not go beyond the deep-seated conviction that those in control of industry should not be "hoggish" in their attitude towards it.[2]

The socialist movement concerns itself primarily with the problem of distribution. It seeks a revolution in

[2] Taylor's declaration that both employers and laborers should be in favor of scientific management, because it would afford larger incomes for both, indicates his failure to appreciate the problem of distribution. Similar views have been perpetuated among his followers. For example, H. L. Gantt states as follows one of three fundamentals in the problem of scientific management; "to find out

economic institutions without a new fundamental point of view. Scientific management concerns itself primarily with production. It seeks to instill a new point of view into productive efforts without bothering itself with the making over of distributive economic institutions.[8]

When we view the work of Taylor with the larger process of cultural development as a background, we get a perspective by which to measure its significance. In spite of the fact that it is fragmentary, dealing only with productive and administrative processes, in spite of the fact that it is not a general social or economic readjustment, scientific management is prophetic in a way that socialism is not, because it is concerned with the viewpoint which is reshaping the existing cultural structure, whereas socialism harks back to an older viewpoint.

STANDARDIZATION AND TECHNICAL IMPROVEMENTS

Development of the current economic situation has meant a great variety of standardizations. Production for wide markets has involved extensive standardization of both production and consumption. The conduct of business in a system which has come to be one vast machine has meant a high degree of standardization of business practices. These and numerous other examples of increasing standardization have come about at a truly

the compensation needed to induce such men to do a full day's work." *Work, Wages, and Profits*, p. 28. This statement ignores entirely the institutional character of the distributive system.

[8] Here, as elsewhere in the present discussion the term distribution refers to the division of economic income and not to the placing of physical goods in the hands of consumers.

astonishing rate because of a relatively high degree of free economic initiative. Because men have been free to adopt new, untried and unstandardized methods, a rapid development of standardization has taken place.[4] So rapidly moving and so pervasive has been the movement towards standardization that the movement itself raises question whither it leads.

A rapid development of technique is so intimate a part of our current economic situation that it has sometimes given rise to a tacit assumption that our economic welfare demands its continuance. One of the stock arguments against capitalistic monopolies is the charge that they retard improvements of technique and thereby are inimical to the public interest. However, the crux of the situation seems to be that the process of standardization must itself bring an end to the rapid rate of technological advance. The fact that capitalistic monopoly results in such retardation is incidental rather than paramount. If the competitive market is losing its authority, is not the argument for competitive pressure to enforce technical improvement losing its significance? The fact that a free play of competitive interests has in the past brought about a rapid and beneficial technical development is no conclusive proof that it will continue to do so. It may

[4] Standardization within the activities of the competitive unit has been especially stimulated by competition. Recent developments through cooperative action, as for example through trade associations, have done much for standardization as between productive enterprises. This latter change has recently received appreciable stimulus from the federal Department of Commerce. *Cf.* the 15th annual report of the Department of Commerce.

TECHNICAL IMPROVEMENTS 169

well be that the future of technological development, such as is to be expected, is dependent upon a process of experimentation which is relatively free from the competitive urge.

The assumption that the public interest is bound up in a continuous process of rapid technological change is, in any case, a gratuitous one. Is technology following an unbroken through trail or a blind alley, or a series of more or less disconnected trails? Can it be expected to continue to change at the pace it has set for the last 150 years or is it headed for a condition of relative perfection, ripeness or maturity which will reduce it to a relatively static condition? While no prediction seems possible at this time as to the extent of its further development in the near future—it may change more in the next 150 years than it has in the last 150 years—yet the logic of the present situation seems to point to a period of technological stability or maturity; that is a maturity of machine technology.[5]

---

[5] The present argument does not afford a place for extended discussion of the proposition that technological development is approaching a period in which technology will be relatively stable or static. The contention is here advanced that technological development is a part of the process of cultural development and not an outside or environmental fact. The rapid development of machine technology during the last 150 years has been an intimate part of a particular cultural development. It has been dependent upon a prevalence of habits of thought tending to foster its development and it in turn has reacted upon those habits of thought, thereby helping to shape them into a dominant philosophical viewpoint. Furthermore such technological development has been the evolution of a particular system of technology. It has not been

The development of a nicely articulated economic organization already has gone so far that even now it operates as a single machine among those peoples who show the most advanced economic development. This has been disclosed by the existence of a business cycle. Business and industrial operations are both parts of this machine and they, as we have seen, are being coordinated through various forms of standardization. Furthermore, the business cycle which is evidence of this vast economic machine is at the same time proof that different parts of the subordinate machinery composing the economic organization are badly articulated. Continuance of the process of cultural standardization may be counted upon to develop a better articulation of parts and thereby to eliminate the business cycle. It is to be expected that the system should eventually reach a condition of relative

merely a section out of an even and undifferentiated process of technological change. The current rapid advance in technology represents an expansion, perfection and filling in of a system of machine technique. Cultural standardization and the standardization of technological processes are inextricably interwoven among peoples making a large use of machine technology. With a higher degree of cultural standardization and a further development of machine technology that interdependence may be expected to increase. It is scarcely to be expected that such a cultural organization as is here implied will forthwith give way to some other. Hence even if so-called Western civilization were to retain its present emphasis upon the economic aspect of human activities, it is scarcely to be expected that an indefinite continuance of the current rapid technological advance would result. And if, as is more likely, a change takes place whereby emphasis is shifted away from the economic aspect of Western culture, the chances for an unbroken advance of technology are rendered much more remote.

stability with respect to both its organization as a whole and the details of technology. The prospect for such a stable economic organization is to be included in the prospect for a régime to supplant the regime of market control.

It would be a mistake to speak of the development of a new economic régime in terms of man's increasing control over the business cycle or of his increasing control over his economic environment. The alternative of a choice between a system of free initiative organized around the open market and a system directed by personal authority as a pilot steers a ship does not exhaust the possibilities. Socialists and orthodox economic theorists are equally at fault in the formulation of such an alternative. Current evidence suggests the near approach of an economic reorganization. But such a new organization, when it comes about, will be one in which men's actions will be subject still to causal determination. A new régime will be neither more nor less natural and neither more nor less final than economic organization around the market has been. Nor will the mechanistic character of the new régime be anything new. The competitive system has been mechanistic notwithstanding the fact that it rested upon a maximum freedom of individual initiative. Differences in the new mechanism which is being developed are in its greater complexity and in its greater coherence, its closer articulation of parts. It will, however, require superhuman or superman guidance neither more nor less than the competitive system.

CULTURAL STANDARDIZATION UPON THE OBJECTIVE VIEWPOINT

To the thesis that a new cultural structure is being shaped under the influence of the machine process and the scientific point of view, it may be offered as an objection that society is too complex and its many aspects too varied to admit of such a summary appraisal of its course of development. Similarly one might well argue that the causes back of the conduct of each individual are so complex and so varied that it would be useless to try to select any fundamental influence, or bias, tending to express unity in the actions of a given individual.

Obviously there are many individuals whose actions show no particular bias or unity. There are others, however, whose actions show a decided tenor or unity which is expressive of some dominant principle or point of view. And so in the history of our civilization there are periods when the institutions making up its cultural structure disclose a unity which is comparable to that which characterizes the actions of most individuals to a greater or less degree. There are other periods when such a unity is scarcely discernible. The evidence appears to indicate that we now are passing through a period of conflict or transition which lacks fundamental unity.

It is true that culture is a very elusive concept, but so is individuality. A particular institution is such an intangible summation of facts that it is difficult to describe it in objective terms. And the word culture stands for a summation or coordination of institutions. But in spite of this cumulative intangibility the term culture does have a definite significance and the process of cultural evolution is not to be gainsaid.

If, on a basis of historical observation and current tendencies, we are willing to risk prediction, past experience points to the conclusion that we are not approaching a final term or goal of cultural evolution. A cultural reorganization upon a basis of the scientific point of view will be no more final than other cultural periods have been. Application of the scientific point of view affords no ultimates, not even the point of view itself. It is a commonplace observation upon cultural development that the radical and subversive principles of one era become the cherished, conservative dogmas of a following era. Time was when the principles of individual liberty and individual initiative were radical and subversive. But now the highest tribunal of this country, the United States supreme court, is a bulwark in defense of those principles. So obvious is this fact that the supreme court becomes a target for criticism by many who are out of sympathy with its point of view even though they have no clear conception of cultural development or of fundamental law. So may we expect some future tribunal, basing its judgments upon the demonstrable results of scientific investigation, to become in its turn a bulwark of conservatism.

The foregoing sounds a little like treason against an authority not yet officially in power, but it is not. In declaring his allegiance to the objective point of view at the beginning of this discussion, the writer had no illusions as to its finality or immutability. Men of former generations have been prone to believe their customs and their religious and political institutions to be perfect, immutable and everlasting. Some take a similar attitude now towards the scientific point of view. There is, however, no particular virtue in such prejudice or short-sightedness. It is quite conceivable that more objectively minded men should be quite ready to die for principles of social organization which they clearly perceive must, in time, be supplanted. One could hardly be convicted of treason in this age, even under a monarchial form of government, for asserting that sometime the king is going to die. The person who holds that science or the scientific point of view is final either as an explanation of experience or as a basis of social organization is as short sighted as was the ardent individualist who once believed that he was struggling to establish, or reestablish, the one divinely instituted order of nature.

SUMMARY

1. Standardization is a necessary part of social organization. It is inevitably prominent in the development of any distinct cultural period.

2. The process of standardization which is now playing so prominent a rôle in human affairs is nothing new. The only distinctive thing about it is the basis upon which it rests.

3. Scientific management is an attempt to apply the objective viewpoint to the problems of production and administration. However, scientific management is not a

large factor in the current situation because it does not cover the entire economic organization. It stands for inculcation of a new viewpoint into productive activities without a reshaping of distributive institutions which went with the old viewpoint. Thus the chief criticism to be offered against it is in a sense the reverse of that offered against the socialist movement.

4. Freedom of economic initiative has brought about a rapid advance of technology and a rapid increase of standardization. Economic organization has become more and more closely welded into one vast machine. The logical conclusion of this line of development is a highly articulated system which may be counted upon to eliminate, to a large degree, both the business cycle and technological change.

5. A cultural organization shaped to fit the scientific point of view is not to be expected to be permanent. Historical example points to the conclusion that the time will come when conservative forces resisting the current of cultural change will base their position upon "objectively determined, demonstrable scientific truth."

CHAPTER XI

NATURE OF LAW AND ITS RELATION TO THE MARKET

When those of us who belong to the so-called Anglo-Saxon group consider our own culture, we sometimes speak glibly of the Dark Ages as if they were for our culture a retrogression. We are proud to have the blood of our barbaric ancestors in our veins. We glory in our biological inheritance from them. But when it comes to cultural matters we are rather prone to disown them as unworthy relations.

As a matter of fact, the line of our cultural inheritance divides. It leads back into the culture of barbaric ancestors as well as to Roman and Greek civilizations. The Dark Ages do not seem so dark when we look back through them into the culture of our tribal forbears. Our own culture rests upon a grafting of much of Roman civilization upon the life of a barbarian stock.

Such graftings are not uncommon in the history of civilizations. They indicate the complexity of elements involved in a given line of cultural descent. Even if it be admitted that our individualistic culture owed its development to the presence of a discipline afforded by a handicraft industrialism, we still must remember that that discipline was only one of many factors shaping the social organization of that period. Other aspects of our cultural heredity are not to be ignored. In the present chapter we are dealing with an important non-economic factor of cultural development.

THE NATURE OF LAW

Law and legal institutions are important parts of the cultural scheme. Because man's experience is fragmentary; because conflicts do arise and their adjustment is a condition of cultural survival, law arises as a basis for the adjustment of conflicting interests and legal institutions arise as means of enforcing the group sanction.

A system of law is, in its formal aspect, a set of rules through which the activities of individuals, and those of groups of individuals, are limited and controlled. Through application to many cases these rules become elaborated and unified. Law eventually becomes systematized. As new cases develop, established rules are applied to them. If the rules for the time and place in which a given case arises are well developed, and the case in question is like those out of which the rules have had their development, no serious difficulty arises. The problem is a mere elementary application of law to a particular case.[1]

If, however, a case arises in which the conflict of interests is different from the run of cases out of which prevailing rules were developed, a serious difficulty is met. There may be no rule which precisely fits the case. One rule of the prevailing system may point to one decision of the issue while another rule in equally good

[1] The term case is not used here in a technical sense which would limit it to a particular system of law. By case is meant any conflict of interests requiring adjustment at law.

standing points to a different decision. Legal authority must effect a reconciliation of this apparent conflict.

As long as exceptional cases are rare, they can be forced into some semblance of ordinary cases without greatly damaging the prestige of the existing legal system. But in a changing cultural situation, exceptional cases sometimes become cumulatively more numerous. If the administration of the law treats them as exceptional cases, and alters the rules accordingly, a process of disintegration sets in. Exceptions multiply and soon destroy the unity and system of the prevailing body of law. But if, on the other hand, the administration of the law treats such cases as if they were not exceptional, violence is done the interests involved and thereby the prevailing system of rules loses prestige. As a result of such a loss of prestige, in a system like our own, public opinion may influence legislative action and subsequent court decisions in such a way as to bring about the disintegration which courts of law in the first instance refused to permit. Or, in particular cases, in our own system of legal institutions, juries may circumvent the law by "finding" facts to be different from what they obviously are. Such action, when it occurs, shows a profound distrust of the law.

Doubtless no formula can be laid down for the evolution of law. It varies greatly in different times and cultures.[2] However, changes in the economic and social conditions of life of a given people necessarily change the

[2] The circumstances cited here as bearing upon the change of law are given because they are pertinent to our own situation. Obviously no general account of legal evolution is intended. For

THE NATURE OF LAW

terms in which their conflicts of interests customarily run. Old principles of adjustment no longer apply. Thereby established legal systems are undermined.[3]

Precisely this sort of a situation now confronts our own culture. It is a recurring situation, and at such a time the law becomes disjointed and uncertain. Not that particular laws are necessarily doubtful or ambiguous. They may not be although they are likely to be so. The rule of reason in anti-trust cases and the complaint of a trial judge cited in Chapter IV [4] are typical illustrations

an extended argument that law does not evolve according to one plan, the reader is referred to Tarde's *Les Transformations du Droit*.

[3] Conclusive evidence that the prevailing system of law does not adequately meet the demands of the current situation is to be seen in the increasing number of boards and commissions whose administrative rulings are given the force of law. "We have always had some degree of individualized application of legal precepts in courts of equity. Today the rise of administrative tribunals and the growing tendency to commit subjects to them that were once committed to the courts, bears witness to the demand for individualized application at many new points. It will not do to say that our new régime of administrative justice is not part of the law." Pound, *Law and Morals*, p. 75.

"We may like it or not, we may hail the recasting of social values or deplore it, but we have to make up our minds that the transformation is taking place as an episode of historical evolution . . . philosophers, naturalists, economists, students of political science, jurists, have all been thinking and talking of evolution. . . . It is time that we should turn to the evolutionary crisis in which we are ourselves implicated nowadays. The ground is shifting under our feet and it is no use pretending that the province of the law alone remains steady and immobile in the midst of the general transformation." Vinogradoff, *Historical Jurisprudence*, Vol. I, pp. 152-53.

[4] P. 82.

of the law's present uncertainty. The uncertainty is, however, much more fundamental than a mere ambiguity of particular statutes or indefiniteness in their application. The whole structure of law breaks loose from its moorings, so to speak, and a new anchorage must be provided for it. More specifically, the philosophy which was the foundation of the prevailing legal system no longer prevails as a common viewpoint characteristic of the group. In the course of time a new philosophy must be interpreted into and under a floating mass of laws, thereby giving them a fundamental foundation and shaping them into a new system of law.

THE PHILOSOPHY OF LAW

The philosophy of law is a changing philosophy. Its function has sometimes been held to be that of placing the law of a given time and place upon a permanent and unchanging foundation. This view is, however, inaccurate. The function of philosophy of law is rather to place the law of a given people upon a foundation which appears to that people and generation to be permanent and unchanging.[5] That is, its function is to rest the law upon the philosophical viewpoint which gives unity to that particular culture.

We are not here interested in the details of the development of different legal systems. A detailed study of the development of the individualistic system of law would

[5] Pound, *An Introduction to Philosophy of Law*, p. 20.

not give us a pattern for later developments.[6] Neither are we interested in the different schools of legal philosophy into which juristic authorities would be divided by a more professional interest. Our concern is rather to show how a new system of law is a necessary part in any general cultural reorganization, and to suggest relationships between the development of such a new system of law and the philosophy which eventually comes to its support.

The formation of a new cultural scheme is truly a multiple process made up of innumerable varieties of cultural standardizations. In the field of technology, based as it is upon the physical sciences, the current process of standardization already is far advanced. Even in the field of social relationships, in matters not confined to a legal strait-jacket, the process is well under way. But so great is the lag in legal development that in it the process of restandardization has hardly begun.

The nature of law is such as to make it ultra-conservative. When the social structure appears otherwise dissolving, law is apt to be most tyrannous and most indispensable. It cannot lead in revolution. So far as the law is concerned, restandardization can come only after cultural standardization has reached a condition of relative stability in other respects.

[6] For a characterization of the formation of the individualistic system of law, see Pound, *An Introduction to the Philosophy of Law*, pp. 41-2. *Cf.* also, Vinogradoff, *Historical Jurisprudence*, Vol. I, p. 157.

Since the rôle of philosophy of law is to relate a given system to an underlying philosophy, it follows that the philosophy of law can make only a very belated appearance. It might be argued that the philosophy of law precedes and guides the formation of a new legal system. The argument has point with respect to the process of systematization of law. Organization is achieved by appeal from less fundamental to more fundamental principles. But growth of the system of law and its systematization are essentially separate periods of its development.[7] A conclusive reason why a new philosophy of law does not develop early is the fact that new law does not typically develop out of old law. Men's habits are more readily shaped at points where they are not subject to the restraint of law. For this reason new rules of conduct typically develop at first unofficially and are absorbed into law only after they have become rather firmly established. Law holds the social structure together while the unofficial and unstandardized activities of men are being moulded into a new system. Hence the essential fallacy of the notion that law, that is the content of a system of law, arises out of the philosophy of law which helps to systematize it.

Discussions of legal philosophy in the latter part of the nineteenth century and at present show the coloring of an evolutionary or objective viewpoint. However, the appearance of that influence is hardly more than a superficial reflection. There is no thoroughgoing application of the objective viewpoint. No one has set out to relate a

[7] Pound, *An Introduction to the Philosophy of Law,* p. 47.

system of law such as that forecast by Dean Pound to prevailing philosophical fundamentals.[8]

When a given system of law holds over beyond the life of the cultural viewpoint with which it originally was associated, it thereby loses its foundation. It comes to be law merely because it is the law. And that is where our legal system now stands. After referring to the divorce of law from ethics by the work of an analytical school of politics, Dean Pound writes as follows:

"Thus the cycle is complete. We are back to the state as the unchallengeable authority behind legal precepts. The state takes the place of Jehovah handing the tablets of the law to Moses, or Manu dictating the sacred law, or the Sun-god handing the code to Hammurabi."[9]

The state is for us the authority behind law but the state is itself now disintegrating. At least it is becoming disorganized and pluralistic. Likewise, and inevitably, the law is breaking down. If, as here argued, a general cultural reorganization is in process, reintegrations of the state and of law are in prospect.

Past experience affords ample basis for the conclusion that whatever social adjustment is effected, there will still be conflicts of interests and legal machinery for their adjustment. However, experience does not tell us in what terms those conflicts will run or the content of legal principles which will be used for their adjustment. Principles of adjustment must develop out of the struggle itself. A new legal system is not to be made out of hand. And as

[8] *Cf.* p. 130 above.
[9] *Law and Morals*, p. 14.

for a new philosophy of law in advance of the new system of law, it is not to be thought of. For the present, all of us must accept current law as so much machinery for adjustment of conflicting interests without looking for an anchorage which it does not have in philosophical fundamentals.[10] We can hope for it to acquire such an anchorage only when the existing cultural scheme is brought into conformity with the viewpoint which is now shaping its development.

LAW AND THE MARKET—EARLY RELATIONS

Market control has not been in any sense a product of legislative action. Speaking metaphorically, the market law of supply and demand was amalgamated with the English common law, but not by any process of legislation. The same cultural situation gave rise to modern representative government, an individualistic system of

[10] "For the purpose of understanding the law of today I am content with a picture of satisfying as much of the whole body of human wants as we may with the least sacrifice. I am content to think of law as a social institution to satisfy social wants—the claims and demands involved in the existence of a civilized society —by giving effect to as much as we may with the least sacrifice, so far as such wants may be satisfied or such claims given effect by an ordering of human conduct through politically organized society. For present purposes I am content to see in legal history the record of a continually wider recognizing and satisfying of human wants or claims or desires through social control; a more embracing and more effective securing of social interests; a continually more complete and effective elimination of waste and precluding of friction in human enjoyment of the goods of existence —in short, a continually more efficacious social engineering." Pound, *An Introduction to Philosophy of Law*, p. 98.

law and a competitive economic organization. The market around which society came to be organized grew out of a market which was not such a focal point of economic organization. This earlier market indisputably was subject to political authority but the change from one market to the other was not a political but a legal adjustment worked out under economic pressure.[11] As long as market adjustments were exceptional rather than the rule, as long as merchants constituted a special and limited class, the administration of the regulations of the market could remain in the non-professional hands of laymen without doing violence to the law, since the scope of the law is general. But when the increasing freedom of individual activity became general, when the process of market adjustment became the general rule, when each individual became potentially a merchant, then a non-professional regulation of market activities became an infringement upon the province of the law.

Whether the immediate impetus to a consolidation of market machinery and legal machinery came from the one side or from the other is immaterial. Even though a militant aggressiveness on the part of common law judges forcibly annexed the law merchant in England, that fact is insignificant. The important consideration is the fact of a fusion of market conventions with the pro-

[11] Schmoller shows the relation of market development to other forms of institutional development and to the development of technique. He describes its development as slow from 1500 to 1850. He emphasizes development of world markets in the nineteenth century, but his interest is from the viewpoint of a circulation of goods. *Grundriss*, etc., Vol. I, p. 21.

fessional law of the land. That process represents the change of the market from a special to a general status.

It well may be pointed out that when regulation by competitive market control was incorporated into the professional law of the land, the function of the law with respect to the market did not thereby become in any respect different from its function in relation to other conduct. In the market, as elsewhere, the business of the prevailing system of law was to permit and to promote a maximum freedom of individual activity.

FURTHER RELATIONS OF LAW TO THE MARKET

Social organization implies a degree of unity—a certain efficiency of mechanical operation. This is true whether it is applied to a small unit or to a cultural group over-reaching national boundaries. The more a group stands out as a distinct unit, the more pronounced its machine-like operation is bound to be. As a given group develops strength it does so through unity and organization rather than through disorganization and conflict. Even if the scheme of organization rests upon a general conflict of interests, as in the competitive system, it still rests upon a more fundamental unity or agreement as to the manner in which conflicting interests are expected to work themselves out to an adjustment.

This mechanistic tendency of social organization has its disadvantages as well as its advantages. The system works well as long as its determining situation remains unchanged. But when changes come, the mechanism of social organization inevitably gives rise to discriminations and injustice. Men are moved to plead, like J. Ramsay MacDonald, for the freeing of men from the tyranny of the machine.

When the law is definitely systematized, it is unified with reference to a given plan or ideal of social organization. At the same time it carries the burden of effecting practical adjustments.[12] For example, the individualistic system of law carried the double burden of preserving individual freedom of action and settling disputes between individuals. One of those functions implies preservation of the prevailing ideal of social organization while the other involves keeping up with the march of a world of changing facts. Thus the law has been driven to attempt to stand still and march forward at the same time. As a consequence it frequently has been guilty of what, in an individual, would be a rank shortcoming in intellectual honesty. It inevitably has become filled with fictions, the tenor of which is to gloss over and minimize social changes bearing upon disputes requiring adjudication.

When the open market was absorbed into the growing system of individualistic law, there thereby devolved upon the law, as part of its wider function of preserving individual liberty, an obligation to keep the market open and competition free. When changing conditions substi-

---

[12] "Evolution in this domain (law) means a constant struggle between two tendencies—the certainty and stability of legal systems and progress and adaptations to circumstances in order to achieve social justice." Vinogradoff, *Historical Jurisprudence*. Vol. I, p. 146.

tuted group interests for much of the individualistic action within the market, the law met the situation by setting up the fictitious individuality of the corporation, thereby bestowing proverbial individual rights upon it. This means that the law pretended to preserve individual action in the market when it in fact did not do so.

More often, however, the law has met changes by ignoring them. This it has sometimes done in decisions affecting labor, as for example in treating the thousands of employees of a corporation, working as they do in widely separated places and for the most part never knowing or seeing each other, as if such a group were comparable to a handful of journeymen working together day after day in the shop of a master workman.

Generally speaking, the law has protected property and the freedom of contract. Those rights are fundamental to the operation of a competitive market. In protecting them the law has indulged in many makeshifts. It was suggested in an earlier connection that even the law has turned against the market. And that statement is to a certain extent true. At the same time, however, the law frequently has been overzealous in its defense of the market. In their service of the two masters above mentioned, that is preservation of an ideal and the effecting of practical adjustments, courts of law, in all probability, have hurt the prestige of the law and the prestige of the market more by a too rigid adherence to the principles underlying the competitive market than by any deflection from them. The law has no more turned against the market than it has turned against itself. The legal protection of the market has suffered just as the law itself has suffered and for the same reasons.

Some of the reasons why the market has lost ground were discussed in Chapter IV. No further argument along that line will be entered into here. The disintegration of market control there presented constitutes one aspect of a disintegration of the individualistic system of law. The process of disintegration has perhaps gone further in connection with the market than it has elsewhere in the law because of the current and recent emphasis upon the economic aspect of our culture. However, the individualistic system of law is just as clearly out of touch with the current cultural situation as is the individualistic market. Both the concrete conditions of life and the prevailing social philosophy which gave rise to an individualistic system of law have changed. Thus both of the foundations of its unity have disappeared. Notwithstanding these facts, there are many persons, including not a small percentage of those trained in the law, who hold that the difficulty in the present situation in the United States is not at all in the law but altogether in a reckless and perverse generation which, on account of prohibition and the late war, has lost all respect for law.

THE PRESENT OUTLOOK FOR LAW

If a cultural reorganization is taking place upon the basis of the scientific point of view; if the social environment of man is to be reshaped by his knowledge of social phenomena just as his physical environment has been altered by his knowledge of physical phenomena; then it follows that the law must be made over in accordance with objective standards. The law must inevitably take its pattern from the cultural régime to which it belongs, just as it did in the development of an individualistic system. A mere "taking more account" of the results of social investigations is not enough.[18] The law must become identified with the point of view which is back of those investigations.

If a particular statute could be so drawn as to rest it upon a direct appeal to the physical senses, it would strike a large majority of the current generation as unassailable. For example those who have tested the effects of modern vaccination by approved quantitative methods accept and insist upon public health regulations providing for vaccination as occasion requires. Indeed they look upon the question as beyond dispute. If any proposed law could be so presented that all members of the group could test it in quantitative terms, as the medical investigator tests vaccination, the result would be a foregone conclusion. It would be flying in the face of science and common sense to question the wisdom of such a proposed law. If an entire system of law were formulated upon such a foundation, the rules of conduct embodied in it would then appear to the present generation to be as unassailable as the laws of physics. And such an appearance of indisputable verity would be nothing new. The eighteenth century individualist thought of the "inalienable rights" of the individual in precisely such terms. Even in the twentieth century it is not unusual to en-

[18] *Cf.* p. 130 above.

counter the tacit assumption that regulation by a competitive market is a necessary and inevitable process of economic adjustment. However, such a common belief in the permanence of a given form of social organization does not establish its permanence.

The current cultural situation affords promise of the development of a system of law based squarely upon the objective point of view. We can look forward with some confidence to what will be in a very significant sense a scientific system of law. But such a system will not represent an end of the evolution of law. There is no guarantee at all as to the length of its duration.

It may appear paradoxical to liken the principles of a scientific system of law to the laws of physics and in the next breath to raise the question of their duration. The contradiction is, however, more apparent than real. Who can guarantee permanence of the vogue of even those formulations which now pass current as the laws of physical sciences? Such laws rest upon a particular philosophical viewpoint. Their prestige is, after all, a cultural fact.

In the absence of a current philosophy of law, the mechanistic character of social organization comes in good stead. As the prevailing but outgrown legal system becomes more and more out of date, the makers and administrators of law are forced to give less and less attention to the preservation of an ideal of social organization while a correspondingly increasing proportion of their attention is given to the practical adjustment of conflicts. At such a time the outstanding legal problem is the working out of a consistent, efficient system of legal principles.

The exigencies of the struggle for survival must be depended upon to fill the rôle of a guiding hand. The social reorganization towards which we are blindly struggling is one in which new institutional machinery will effect social adjustments with a resulting general satisfaction because such adjustments rest upon grounds which are generally accepted. When such a reorganization is achieved, the emphasis of legal administration will shift again from the making of practical adjustments to the preservation of an ideal. Then a new legal philosophy will be but an aspect of the new social organization which administrators of the law will be called upon to preserve.

SUMMARY

1. The rise of the free market was part of the rise of a distinct system of law and the decadence of the market is likewise a part of the disintegration of that same legal system.

2. The passing of the individualistic period of our culture involves the passing of this individualistic system of law and its eventual supersession by another system.

3. Notwithstanding its many makeshifts and its lack of straightforward honesty, the law has not been able to preserve the ideal of a social order based upon the principle of a maximum freedom of individual initiative.

4. Philosophy of law serves to relate a given system of law to an underlying philosophical viewpoint. In a transition period characterized by disorganization and conflict in the various spheres of human activity, the law enters upon a transition stage. It finds itself without a funda-

mental philosophical foundation and, in the nature of the case, it can not have one under such circumstances.

5. But when a social reorganization has been more fully worked out; when new customs making up that reorganization have become established; when new habits and new routines have become relatively fixed in human conduct, then a new system of law and a new philosophy of law will appear. Cultural readjustment may be counted upon to provide both a new social ideal and new legal machinery for the preservation of that ideal.

CHAPTER XII

THE MARKET AND ACCOUNTS

The mechanism of a competitive market was peculiarly adapted to a situation in which a high degree of flexibility was necessary. The market's most efficient operation requires numerous competing buyers and sellers. Under such conditions, particular individuals may drop out or new ones appear without in any way impairing the efficiency of the market mechanism. It will continue to function while admitting of constant disturbance. In fact, the most realistic description of the market pictures it as a composite of numerous disturbing causes which never work themselves out to a stable equilibrium before new ones enter into the complex. It is this characteristic which has made the market an institution peculiarly suited to a period of rapid economic development.

LIMITATIONS OF THE MARKET

Since the market's operation is a continuous process of adaptation, since it is called upon at all times to make allowance for disturbing causes, its decisions can not be other than approximations. Flexibility is afforded it at the cost of exactness. It is not an instrument of exact measurement.

Both in theory and in practical fact the market rests upon choices of individuals between different lines of action. This being the case, exact measurements by the market mechanism are out of the question. The influences bearing upon human conduct have never been reduced to exact measurement; not even to the extent of expression in objective terms. In the absence of an explanation of choice in such terms, conduct commonly is dealt with in economics in frankly subjective terms. When it is so treated, choice becomes a matter of the harmonization and organization of ends rather than a matter of the relative magnitude of measurable phenomena.

The market was highly suited to a pioneer society carrying on a more or less rough and tumble competitive process of development. In a situation requiring frequent proximate decisions rather than nicely calculated adjustments, it worked admirably. But it has not fitted in so well with a more highly complex economic situation in which more exact instruments of measurement are required.

An analogy is to be drawn between the development of technology and the development of institutional equipment like the market. In handicraft industry a workman was known by his tools. If he used good tools and kept them in good condition, they gave promise of a workmanlike character in his product. It was a common saying that good tools make a good workman. Better tools, other things equal, made possible a nicer articulation of the workman's efforts and a better product. But the development of industrial technique has not been confined to providing the handicraftsman with better tools. Machine processes have made possible incomparably more minute workmanship than the handicraftsman ever could have achieved no matter how good his tools.

A somewhat similar line of development is to be observed with respect to institutional machinery. As an increasingly complex society has required more exact economic adjustments, they have been afforded, in a limited degree, by improvements in the prevailing variety of institutional equipment for effecting such adjustments. But in time new institutional equipment is bound to be required to accomplish results not attainable by the old technique. It is perhaps characteristic of the process of cultural development that institutional reorganization has not kept pace with technological change. The conservative tendency of the law has led it to go on refining and revising the machinery of the market in an attempt to preserve its efficiency as a practical means of adjusting conflicting economic interests. Many economists have followed the lead of the law and have set up progressively more and more detailed refinements of the theoretical analysis of a competitive market. They commonly have found exactness of measurement when in fact there was no exactness afforded by the workings of the market. If the analogy here drawn between technology and market machinery holds good, the time must come when both legal authorities and economists must recognize that the competitive market is only a rough tool suited particularly to the needs of a pioneer age.

EARLY RELATIONS OF ACCOUNTS TO THE MARKET

Accounts and the market have not by any means maintained a constant relation to each other. Although the market has changed greatly, accounts have changed even more. The market became stereotyped by official recognition. Its incorporation into law made it authoritative. Thereby it became the formally accepted machinery for adjustment of conflicting economic interests.

In their development accounts have not been handicapped by any such official responsibility, although in their early history they were even more circumscribed than the market itself. In the field of merchandising in which accounting first developed, the scope and function of accounts were limited, in the beginning, to recording decisions rendered by the market. A system of books constituted a record of transactions affecting one particular competitive interest. The theory of accounts involved nothing beyond setting up an efficient bookkeeping record. Accounting was, thus, entirely subordinate to the market and to law. The influence of this early subordinate and wholly dependent position still is dominant in accounting literature. That literature is only now emerging from the influence of its early environment.

CHANGES IN THE MARKET AND IN ACCOUNTS

The developments of modern business enterprises greatly changed the situation in which the market has served its functions. Machine processes have meant technological operations on a relatively large scale. The administration of such operations has necessitated a continuity of control not afforded by individualistic ownership and management. As a result, forms of group ownership and group control have developed. This has meant a very great change in the typical competitive unit in the market. In accepted legal and economic theory the market has remained the same, thanks to the legal fiction of individuality attached to new forms of group interests appearing in it. In reality, however, the market became thereby a very different thing. A market dominated by large super-corporate enterprises, each of which is managed upon a basis of selection between long run policies, is quite different from a market dominated by individualistic competitive interests.

When the typical competitive unit in the market became a composite unit, a double duty devolved upon accounts. Growth of the system of accounts needs must keep pace with the growth of the competitive unit in order to preserve a record of its interests as against those of other like units. At the same time accounts were called upon to distinguish between subordinate interests within the composite unit.

In spite of its flexibility, the machinery of the market could not be depended upon to adjust conflicts between partnership interests, or all the possible conflicts of interests between creditors and stockholders, or those between preferred stockholders and common stockholders. Partnership law, corporation law and modern trust legislation have all grown up out of changes in the market. For the most part they have grown out of the fundamental change which the law in the first instance met by setting up a fictitious individuality of group interests. When the market has failed to effect satisfactory adjustments in a changing situation, the law and accounts have been drawn in to supplement it and to round out a complete system for the settlement of conflicting economic interests.

The double duty here shown to devolve upon accounts, by reason of the evolution of the market, is only part of the story. The increasing size and complexity of the competitive unit changed the problem of business administration. When an individual represented the typical unit in the market, and enterprise was carried on in a comparatively small way, the individual businessman's attention was directed chiefly to problems involving his economic relationships to other competitive units. Accounting was mainly a record of those relationships. The record function of accounts stood out almost to the exclusion of other functions. But when the operation of the competitive enterprise became a highly complex, closely articulated and relatively continuous process, the problems of administration were greatly changed. Problems of internal management and control came to have an importance comparable to that attaching to external problems of purchase and sale. Various factors of internal and external relationships could not be handled in a consistent, effective administration without expression in some sort of common terms. Accounting was the means at hand to furnish that expression. Hence the development of internal accounts and the control function of accounts, thereby affording management a new and indispensable technique.[1]

ILLUSTRATIVE ACCOUNTING PROBLEMS

The functional changes which have taken place in accounts during the course of their development are best illustrated by reference to specific problems. For example, the reporting of profits from business operations is one of the outstanding services of accounts. In the case of early trading companies, which bought goods at home for transport abroad in their own ships with a view to bringing back foreign goods for sale at home, the relationships involved were very simple. Whether a particular venture was profitable or not was easily determined. In fact the market determined the matter fairly directly by fixing the purchase and sale prices of goods involved. The margin of profit in such enterprises frequently was enhanced by judicious trading in countries where there were no competitive markets. Sometimes the market at home was not competitive with respect to the goods imported. But these considerations did not interfere with the relative simplicity of the necessary accounting procedure. The goods involved in each venture were, in time, turned into cash or charged off to the cost of the venture. Net proceeds from the undertaking were obvious.[2]

It is a long way from such a primitive statement of

[1] Bliss, *Management Through Accounts*, Ch. I.
[2] Brown, *History of Accounts and Accountants*, p. 115.

ILLUSTRATIVE ACCOUNTING PROBLEMS

profits to the operating report of a modern manufacturing company producing upon a large scale. The manufacturing company carries on, more or less continuously, a great many operations upon each of which it is not possible to determine separately a profit. When any statement of profits is to be made, it is prepared upon a basis of a given fiscal period rather than upon specific operations. The condition of fixed properties, numerous items of expenses paid in advance, expenses accrued not paid, depreciation accrued and many other considerations must be taken into account in the determination of net income or net loss. All the problems of income and expense accrual are involved in such a periodic determination of profits. In short, the development of large scale operations in the field of production has made the accounting for such enterprises a complex and difficult matter requiring the formulation and application of principles which had no place in the early competitive régime in which accounts first developed.

The point here to be emphasized is not so much the greater complexity which large scale production has brought into accounting problems, but rather the change which it has caused in accounting functions. If a given manufacturing company has non-cumulative preferred stockholders as well as common stockholders, accounting is called upon to draw the line of division between their interests. The market does not automatically adjust this conflict. The market does not determine whether a profit was earned during a given fiscal period.

Similarly, accounting, rather than the market or the

law, draws the line between the interests of present stockholders and those of future stockholders. Of course the market fixes the price at which present stockholders sell to future stockholders, in so far as the stock is sold, but even in such sales the bids behind the resultant market price commonly rest upon accounting reports of profits earned and asset values. The principles of accounting, principles of law, accounting technique and the machinery of the market are all mixed up together in the process by which conflicting interests are adjusted. Lines drawn between accounting principles and legal principles, or between accounting technique and market technique, are arbitrary. All are closely related parts of the current economic structure.

Perhaps the best illustration of how the adjustment of conflicting economic interests has come to be dependent upon accounts is in the regulation of public utilities. Issues involving rates charged and profits allowed require an accounting basis for their settlement. In its decisions aiming at justice as between investors and consumers, the regulating commission is as much dependent upon accounts as is the manager of any competitive enterprise; more so in fact, if that is possible. But whether we consider competitive business or regulated enterprise, accounting has become an intimate part of the current machinery of economic control.

CHANGED PROBLEM OF ACCOUNTING RECORD

The typical accounting record has come to be a record not of one but of many interests. The relationships to

CONTROL FUNCTION OF ACCOUNTS

be recorded and differentiated are many and various. Creditors, and customers, profit-sharing managers and employees, present and future stockholders, common and preferred stockholders, majority and minority stockholders, partners, bond holders and underwriters represent some of the interests involved in modern enterprise. They present themselves in a limitless variety of combinations. As a result, individual business transactions have come to have a different significance from what they had in a simpler system because they now have bearing upon a greater variety of interests. The question of their proper treatment has therefore come to be a much more difficult question. This change has greatly influenced the development of accounting forms. The technique of the accounting record has undergone a great deal of development which has been made necessary by the increasing complexity of business organization. But of much greater significance is the development of accounting theory whereby the treatment of business transactions is so governed as to protect the increased variety of interests at stake in competitive and regulated enterprises.

THE CONTROL FUNCTION OF ACCOUNTS

The control function of accounts is well illustrated in the statement that they serve to connect and to unify technological operations and the business administration which controls and directs production. The bare fact that particular accounting systems are constructed with a view to their serving the needs of management shows how important this control function has become. As the typical business unit has developed in size and complexity, its continued growth has been dependent upon a corresponding development in accounting principles and accounting technique. Cost accounting, in all of its guises, is a phase, but only one phase, of this development.

When the unit of business control has overreached the limits of the corporate form of organization, accounting has kept pace with it in the development of consolidated accounts. The preparation of periodic consolidated statements involves the keeping of continuous supplementary records and the result is the development of a super-corporate system of accounts.

Consolidated accounts must deal with problems which do not arise in the relatively simple affairs of the single independent corporation. The equities of minority stockholders in subsidiary companies and the complications which arise from a mixture of partnerships and corporations give rise to some of these problems. Accounting technique and principles to cover consolidated accounts, or a super-corporate accounting system, have not yet developed as far as the technique and principles accounting for the conduct of business by the simpler form of corporate organization. But neither has the management of super-corporate business organizations developed to a degree comparable to that of corporate management. Super-corporate management and super-corporate accounting are both in relatively early stages of development. They wait upon each other.

The essential point in the foregoing discussion is that accounting functions and accounting forms are in process of development and that both of them are intimately involved in the process by which conflicting economic interests are adjusted. It follows as a logical conclusion from this argument that the manner in which such economic interests are adjusted is itself in course of development.

DEPENDENCE OF ACCOUNTS UPON THE MARKET

The history of accounting development discloses a growth of accounting functions, an increasing dependence of business administration upon accounts and the absorption of accounting technique into the body of social machinery through which conflicting economic interests are adjusted. It has been stated that the maximum responsibility placed upon accounts is to be found in the government regulation of public utilities. Accounting furnishes government commissions their chief tool of regulation. It affords them both a technique of control and principles of adjustment. But even in this connection, accounting has not escaped dependence upon the superior control of the market. Unless authority is given to a commission to take the place of the market in the direction of the existing economic system as a whole it must continue to be so dependent. Regulation in particular fields has become steadily more and more positive. But in any case the limitation of such regulation to a particular jurisdiction makes it the exception in an unregulated system. When a commission is authorized to regulate a given industry so as to attract a desired amount of capital to that industry and to assure such capital a reasonable rate of return, there is a background of unregulated industries assumed, in which returns are competitive and therefore reasonable, and from which capital is to be attracted to the regulated industry. Hence both the regulating commission and the system of accounts which it utilizes are still dependent upon the competitive market. We can safely generalize to the effect that in a competitive system accounting must always remain thus dependent upon the market. It must look to the market as to a superior authority.

However, the market, as we have seen, is losing its authority. Accounts, on the other hand, are steadily increasing in importance. What will happen if regulation becomes the rule rather than the exception and the authority of the competitive market dwindles into relative insignificance?

Accounting has developed under the dominance of market control. In spite of the increasing functions served by accounts and their more nearly universal use, they have remained subordinate to the market. If, as here suggested, market control, as a fundamental basis of economic organization, is to be cast into the discard of outworn institutions, will it carry accounting with it to the scrap heap? The purpose of the present chapter is to raise this question rather than to answer it.

SUMMARY

1. The market is a rough tool suited to the needs of a pioneer age. In such a situation it effected approximate adjustments with admirable efficiency.

2. But in a social situation requiring exact measurements, the market must be supplanted by other institutional equipment just as the handicraftsman's tools have been supplanted by machine processes.

3. In their early history, accounts merely recorded decisions of the market. They were entirely subordinate to the market and to law.

4. However, more and more of the responsibility for effecting economic adjustments has come to be shared between accounts and the market. At the same time accounts have developed into a position of importance as an instrument of administrative control.

5. The steadily increasing importance of accounts has been coupled with a declining significance of the market. And yet accounts still are dependent upon the market. Is this dependence a necessary and unavoidable relationship? If the market becomes a subordinate institution, will accounts still be subordinate to it?

These questions stand as yet unanswered.

CHAPTER XIII

ACCOUNTS AND STATISTICS

Discussion of the relations of accounts to the market in Chapter XII was, for the most part, a treatment of functions served by accounts. In the present chapter, discussion of the relations of accounts to statistics will deal, for the most part, with the development of accounting technique.

A COMMON VIEWPOINT

Writers in the field of accounting have sometimes discussed the place of statistics in accounts. In such discussions the term statistics refers to various compilations of data running sometimes in money terms and sometimes in other terms but never forming part of the content of the record which is indirect line to be summed up in the balance sheet and the income statement. This distinction between the double entry record and records outside the double entry system rests upon the assumption that accounting is, after all, the double entry record. Other statistical data are characterized as supplementary adjuncts of the accounting system rather than as fundamentally parts of it.

Those who conceive economic theory to be a rigid system built up deductively on the basis of a few fundamental generalizations are not without their counterparts in the field of accounting. For example, the author of a recently published elementary text writes as follows:

ACCOUNTING DEVELOPMENT

"Accounting is not an end but a tool for the interpretation and the direction of business. The student who grasps this truth will perceive that the methods and applications of accounting must vary to meet diverse demands and conditions. Yet all sound accounting is based on a few fundamental principles and conventions which can be mastered and then developed to fit particular cases." [1]

The position to be taken in this chapter is contrary to the foregoing view. It will be argued here that the so-called statistical materials included in the records of modern business enterprises are just as intimately and necessarily a part of current accounting systems as is double entry technique itself. It will be contended that accounts are not identical with the double entry record and that any definition of them based upon the double entry record is too narrow to be applicable to the accounting for current business affairs.

ACCOUNTING DEVELOPMENT

As students of accounts are well aware, the double entry system of accounts developed from records of debtor and creditor relationships.[2] The introduction of other types of ledger accounts into the system came about gradually. We are not here interested in the details of the development of different classes of ledger accounts or even in the expansion and multiplication of

---

[1] From the preface to *Elementary Accounting*, by Frank H. Streightoff.

[2] Brown, *History of Accounts and Accountants*, p. 94.

journal and ledger forms. All such formal developments of technique have come out of the application of the double entry system to actual business affairs. They are here taken for granted.

The same experience which gave rise to developments of double entry technique gave rise also to numerous rules or principles governing the application of that technique to particular cases. Accounting theory had its origin in accounting practice. When the scope and functions of accounting technique expanded in a changing economic organization, an enhanced significance thereby attached to the formulated principles governing accounting practice. Men skilled in an understanding of those principles and in their application to practical business affairs gradually acquired a status akin to that of the older professions. Accountants came to be regarded as something more than mere grown-up bookkeepers.

The foregoing simple analysis is far from complete. In attempting to apply principles governing the use of double entry records to modern business affairs, accountants have been compelled to rely more and more upon statistical records not included in the double entry system. Our task in the present chapter is to consider the significance of this encroachment of statistics upon accounting territory. Why this dependence upon statistics? What bearing does this increasing use of statistical methods have, first, upon the double entry record, and second, upon accounting theory which initially has developed as a body of principles relating to the use of the double entry record?

STATISTICS IN ACCOUNTS

Accounting data in the double entry record cover a great many and a great variety of business facts. The interpretation of this record by business men is essentially a statistical interpretation. Expense analyses, cost ratios and profits percentages are statistical concepts. Double entry records themselves constitute a variety of statistical data. Since statistics is the broader term we might better turn the above topic heading around and discuss the place of accounts in statistics. However, that would not suit present purposes so well as the more usual statement since we are concerned with an increasing use in accounts of materials not included in the double entry record.

The incorporation of statistical technique into accounts has resulted from an increasing complexity of business problems. For example, the use of accounting records to determine the profits of a modern enterprise is possible only upon the basis of statistical technique. It involves the application of numerous principles connected with the accrual of expense and income. One of the problems of cost determination is the allocation of depreciation. Such allocation has come to be an accounting problem but it is dependent upon statistical records outside the double entry system. Whatever the method chosen for determination of periodic depreciation charges, we are involved in the necessity of making a statistical calculation based upon records of previous experience. The average service life of a given type of asset can be obtained only in that way. And the more accurate we seek to be, the more we are drawn into the statistical aspect of the problem.

The foregoing illustration could be matched by numerous others connected with cost allocation—fire risk, accident liability and the like. However, the encroachment of statistics upon the accounting field is best illustrated from a more general viewpoint. Students trained along the line of double entry records alone are apt to be very much at sea when confronted by the accounting system of a large enterprise. A multiplicity of forms, the distribution of records over many departments, the summarization of data in statements which do not take the form of balance sheets and income statements and the keeping of records which do not run in money terms, are all parts of a system calculated to afford a maximum of information useful for the purposes of administrative control. In such a system the question whether a given record is a journal or a ledger, or both, or neither, gets scant consideration. Some records obviously belong in the double entry system while others obviously do not. Still others are so woven into a system of journals and ledgers that it would be quite useless to try to draw an exact line of division between the part of the system which is the double entry record and the part which is outside of the double entry record. In fact the double entry record has been absorbed into a more comprehensive system which derives its unity from functions served rather than from a rigid formalism.

Industrial accounts afford perhaps the best illustration

of the change here under discussion. The rise of manufacturing upon a large scale brought about a separation, or at least a poor coordination, between industrial processes and business management. Relatively independent systems of control of the two developed. Inefficiency arising from such an absence of effective coordination eventually gave rise to the introduction of cost accounts. In their early form cost accounts constituted a relatively independent system of control over technical operations. They necessarily involved much statistical material not running in money terms. Practical experience, however, soon proved the unworkableness of an independent system of cost accounts. Two independent records made the situation more complex rather than less so. Unified machinery of control was and is an obvious necessity but it was not to be achieved in that way. The advantages of centralization impelled a unification of all accounting records. This inevitable unification has come about, not through the absorption of cost records into the system of commercial accounts, or vice versa, but rather, through the absorption of both into a single more comprehensive system which is essentially different from the old double entry record. And it is this latest form of accounting record which is tending to bridge the gap between industrial operations and the business management controlling them.

THE MANAGEMENT FUNCTION AND ACCOUNTS

Management of an industrial enterprise involves the coordination of a great many processes. Problems of finance, the purchase of labor, purchase of materials and equipment, the production and sale of finished products and many other more detailed operations are all involved in a single undertaking. Since the introduction of machine processes has made manufacturing a relatively continuous process—a process which moves forward with a considerable degree of momentum—it has become of paramount importance to keep operations running smoothly. Friction tends to be cumulative and to multiply costs. A centralization of authority is necessary to keep down friction and keep up the momentum of operations. Nor is a formal centralization of authority sufficient. The central management must exercise continual foresight to anticipate difficulties and solve them before they disturb the regular routine. This forward-looking characteristic of modern management is no less significant than the necessity for coordination of numerous concurrent operations. The manager must keep a sharp lookout on all sides and a clear view of the road ahead, like a man driving a car in heavy traffic. Both the nice coordination of concurrent processes and the importance of the look ahead are largely by-products of the machine process.

In order that management may be able to forecast coming events and thereby maintain a continuous coordination of activities, a comprehensive and continuously replenished fund of information about the enterprise is necessary. Obviously the system for assembling this information must be unified and comprehensive. It must assemble data upon which the plans of an intelligent management can be safely based. At the same time it must serve as the means of checking up on operations to see that plans made and orders issued are being carried out.

Industrial accounting is confronted by conditions which are more complicated than those covered by other fields of accounting. Control over the actual process of production requires physical and accounting control over materials and labor. It requires similar control over equipment and a working control over technical processes. The bringing together of materials, labor, equipment and technique involves a multitude of variable factors. Labor is subject to substitution within certain limits and is freely mobile from one to another of similar jobs. Given equipment may be useful in a number of different ways. A choice of processes often is possible in achieving a given result. Certain processes may need to be adapted to the character and quality of a given lot of raw material. There may be a choice of alternative materials in making a given product. The routing of materials, the rotation of processes performed upon them and the combination of products worked upon at any given time afford additional bases of variation. Many others could be enumerated. Thus the actual management of a manufacturing enterprise involves a continuous multiple correlation between choices of materials, labor, equipment, processes and products. And no one of them all is itself a constant for any considerable length of time. With these facts in mind, one should not be surprised that the quantity production of one product, or of a small line of highly standardized products, has stood out so prominently in the early history of the machine process.

The quantity production of highly standardized goods has not been dependent solely upon the machine process. It has been furthered greatly by improvements in accounting methods and accounting records. Such improvements in accounting have pushed the margin of effective control further and further into industrial processes which do not lend themselves readily to simplification.

Industrial accounts, as a whole, have not yet reached such a stage of development that they show a high degree of standardization.[8] Nevertheless, from the viewpoint of their service as an instrument of control they represent the most advanced development of accounting to date. The successful incorporation into them of a large percentage of statistical technique is exercising a decided influence in other fields of accounting. For example, developments in the field of merchandising enterprise show distinctly an influence of this character. Merchandising operations were largely responsible for the original development of double entry technique. But industrial operations are, to a large degree, responsible for a making over of the accounting system to include a maximum of statistical technique. Following the leadership of the industrial field, trading enterprises are developing systems

[8] The trend which is taking place in the direction of a standardization of industrial accounts is indicated in the work of industrial accountants. *Cf.* Woods, *Unified Accounting Methods for Industrials.*

similar to industrial accounts. The large retail store is rapidly taking on a factory-like aspect. Thus the system of accounts which includes a maximum of statistics and subordinates double entry technique is becoming general.[4]

A DEFINITION OF ACCOUNTS

Like other institutional machinery, accounting technique came into use before the development of theoretical generalizations associated with it. Double entry arose before the formulation of a body of accounting theory. With the development of principles and their application to particular cases, accounting theory and accounting technique became clearly defined and contrasted concepts. But in the course of its further use, under changing conditions of business affairs, accounting technique has come to accord a prominent place to new forms of statistical data. The accounting record has become so comprehensive that the concepts of the journal and the ledger no longer typify the accounting system of a large enterprise. Can such a change as this take place in accounting technique without inducing an equally significant change in accounting theory? Surely not. And yet when we still define accounting and accounting theory in terms of the double entry record, we assume that no such change has taken place in either one of them. Surely we can do no

[4] Railway managements made use of a great deal of statistical information far in advance of the development of modern industrial accounts. Usage in that field, however, appears to have been too limited and too specialized to exert a general influence such as industrial accounts have since exercised.

less than say that accounting theory concerns itself with theoretical formulations governing the application of double entry technique plus a certain amount of other statistical technique. But just how much statistics is to be included?

As we have seen, it has become impossible in many cases to separate double entry from the rest of the accounting record. Even the terms debit and credit have been pretty well swamped by the increasing variety of records. They still take a prominent place in the system of accounts but they have long since lost their realistic connotation and have become merely statistical terms. Hence the simple and direct thing to do seems to be to say that accounting theory is a body of principles governing the application of statistical methods to business administration, including the problem of differentiation of interests at stake in business enterprise. Accounting is, undeniably, a subordinate branch of statistics. Why, if not, should the fact not be recognized in a theoretical discussion of accounts?

It is now common practice for a large enterprise to have both accounting and statistical departments. It is easy to understand why this should be so. It has been easier to create a new department to render certain statistical services than to make over a department which was already functioning in an established manner. The line of least resistance has been followed. However, the essential unity of the service performed by the two departments must eventually lead to their amalgamation just as commercial accounts and cost accounts have been amalgamated.

FURTHER INFLUENCES OF THE MACHINE PROCESS

By reducing business and industrial operations to routine, the machine process has given rise to the necessity for an administration, or control, which expresses itself through the formulation and execution of relatively long run policies. Forecast has come to be a routine function of management. This especial emphasis upon prediction we have seen has come about as a product of the machine process. It is one of the important immediate factors tending to enforce the change in attitude of business management discussed at length in Chapter VIII.

With respect to the immediate character of the management function, the machine process has made necessary both a greater concentration and a continuity of control. The form of this control already has been described. It involves ability to shape conditions for subordinates so that orders can be carried out. It requires a checking up on operations to show whether orders are being carried out, and if not, it requires action to prevent failure at one point from interfering with operations at other points.

But no business management is omnipotent. There are things affecting its administration which it cannot control. Sources of raw materials, markets for sale of products, general business conditions, and many special conditions within the industry to which the enterprise belongs, are all more or less outside the control of the management. Hence, while a management controls and coordinates operations within the business unit which it administers, it must also correlate those operations with factors which it does not control. The competitive notion of a society organized through a control by the market over the expenditure of economic efforts is no longer realistic. The manager who depends upon the market to guide him is now out of date. Equally out of date is the manager who depends upon his hunches and general experience to tell him what the market is going to do. The current emphasis upon prediction has impelled management to cut across lots and adjust itself to more fundamental factors bearing upon the market which it serves.[5] Thus where the form of the competitive market has been

[5] "It is foresight that business men ask for today; anyone knows what has happened in the past. The better the foresight exercised by executives and managers in the control of industries, the more stable will business conditions become. As business managers come to a better understanding of the fundamental changes and general business conditions, particularly those affecting their own industry, they will be in a better position to meet these changing business conditions and adjust the affairs of their companies accordingly, with a minimum of inconvenience and loss. This point is apparent in the everyday conversations of business men now as compared with pre-war times. Today we hear freely discussed various phases of the business cycle, changes in underlying economic conditions, foreign relations, foreign trade and exchange, and such other topics little thought of by the average business man before the war. In short, business today is more scientific than ever before, and requires a better understanding of underlying economic conditions." Bliss, *Management Through Accounts*, p. 42.

preserved, much of the adjustment traditionally credited to the market already has been effected before products are actually brought to the market. Furthermore there is a constantly increasing tendency in this direction. And the tendency takes an added significance when it is considered in connection with the fact that an increasing percentage of economic activity is carried on either directly under government regulation or by what Prof. Bruce Wyman has called "public businesses."[6]

It may be well at this point to repeat from earlier discussions by way of appraising the relationships of accounting and business management. It is illuminating to refer to three distinct phases of historical development. In the early development of double entry accounts they were primarily a tool of business enterprise in the field of trading or merchandising. Bargaining, or the operations of purchase and sale, played a relatively large rôle in such forms of enterprise. Accounting was essentially a record of the results of bargaining.

A second phase in the relationship between accounting and management is to be seen in the development of internal accounts. This change in accounts reflects a shift of emphasis on the part of management from bargaining to internal administration. It resulted in emphasis upon the control function of accounts. This second phase is to be credited to the extension of business enterprise to control of processes of production. And the rôle of business enterprise in production is to be credited largely, though not wholly, to the development of machine processes.

[6] *Control of the Market*, Ch. V.

At the present time, we are in still a third phase of business enterprise or management. The emphasis of management is again shifting to external relationships, not however to the process of bargaining in the market. It has become a definite goal of management to coordinate the operations of the business enterprise with factors which the management does not control. An objective or factual basis for the determination of policies is the means through which this desired goal can be achieved. External coordination and internal control have come to have a common foundation in a statistical interpretation of pertinent facts.

Skillful management of business enterprise now involves a balance or coordination between internal administration, the management of relations to debtors and creditors, and an adjustment to environmental conditions. Past developments indicate that the competitive struggle for survival will hasten the further development of such balanced or unified managements.

Such a balanced management must have, as a working tool, a unified system of records. Hence the above prediction that accounting and statistical departments must eventually be amalgamated.

A suggestive analogy is to be drawn between the evolution of the individual and evolution of the unit of business enterprise. When individuals become more capable of adjusting themselves to environmental circumstances, a more complex form of social organization is possible. In fact, the development of such capacity on the part of individuals and the development of a more complex social organization are simultaneous.

Similarly, the development of units of business enterprise which are increasingly capable of adjusting themselves to environmental conditions makes possible a more complex economic organization. Indeed, the development of an increasingly complex economic organization is taking place simultaneously with the development of the capacities of the business unit.[7] And further, this increased complexity and power of adjustment on the part of the individual business unit cannot take place without a comparable change in economic organization at large. A South Sea islander could not become a civilized individual without the development of a civilized society.

SUMMARY

1. Accounting theory developed as a body of rules or principles governing the application of double entry records in the conduct of business affairs.

2. But changed conditions of business affairs have so altered the functions served by accounts that accounting is no longer merely a double entry record. The double entry record has become submerged in a system organized from a functional point of view. A redefinition of accounting in terms broader than the double entry system is therefore necessary.

[7] *Cf.* W. C. Mitchell's statement as to the type of management which is now typical. *Business Cycles, The Problem and Its Setting*, p. 157.

3. To meet the demands made upon it under the complex conditions of modern business enterprise, the accounting system has been made progressively more flexible and more comprehensive through the introduction of statistical procedure. Now it stands virtually as an application of statistical methods within a limited field. At least, that is the point towards which it appears to be rapidly moving.

4. Through the use of more efficient accounting and statistical technique, the unit of business enterprise is acquiring an increasing capacity for adjustment to environmental circumstances. This development is both evidence of and a basis for an increasingly complex economic organization.

CHAPTER XIV
GOVERNMENT, ACCOUNTS AND THE MARKET

Confused and inconsistent thinking about law and government is characteristic of current popular discussions. This malady, if it may be so called, is illustrated by the argument of a certain pair of estimable citizens and fellow clubmen. These two gentlemen agreed that the mere enactment of legislation does not make law; that formal legislation requires support in which the weight of community opinion counts for much more than police power or the sheriff's authority. With respect to prohibition, one of them argued that police forces, sheriffs and special agents combined had been unable to enforce the law because public opinion was not behind it. The other, however, insisted that prohibition had been reasonably well enforced by the weight of public opinion in spite of the fact that its enforcement had been largely in the hands of political appointees not in sympathy with its enforcement.

When the conversation chanced to shift to international law and the world court, these two gentlemen were again in agreement that such so-called law and such a court could at best be nothing more than academic conceptions because, forsooth, there are no supernational policemen and sheriffs.

The unusual degree of confusion and contradiction now

to be observed in discussions of government and politics is to be attributed to the fact that political institutions are in a condition of more than ordinary flux. Of course they are always in a flux but not always to the same extent.

Government is only a practical makeshift—a mere *modus vivendi*. A government which is the product of revolution gains respectability in a remarkably short time. Styles in government come and go without apparent prejudice to the prestige of the current form. Political philosophers commonly have followed the current style and have invested sovereignty in the ruling monarch, parliament or the people, as the case might be. Or in default of better material, they have set up a fictitious state personality comparable to the legal personality of the corporation.

Of late some political scientists have forsaken the presentation of political theory from the viewpoint of an undivided sovereignty and have betaken themselves to the task of describing in a more realistic and objective fashion how governments arise out of the practical adjustment of conflicting interests. This method has brought into relief the evolutionary character of government.

An outstanding governmental change now in process in the United States is a rapid increase of burdens resting upon the federal government. This change is being brought about in part through economic changes. Lines of distinction between purely economic matters and governmental affairs are breaking down. Economics and politics are together becoming a first class hodge-podge. It is becoming more and more difficult for the economist and the political scientist to maintain their special abstractions. And those separate abstractions are becoming correspondingly less significant notwithstanding the greater effort which they cost. In this respect the current situation has reached a critical stage and continues to grow worse.

Doubtless, after the present interregnum, the political scientist and economist will find themselves with brand new sets of abstractions. But in the meantime we are confronted by a seemingly inescapable and irresistible course of development which is multiplying the duties and obligations of government. The import of this development for government is a matter of immediate and paramount importance. Our interest here is in its immediate significance and not in the long run prospect of new sets of political and economic abstractions. What is likely to be the effect of this current trend upon the evolution of government? What is to precede the formulation of new abstractions by the economist and political scientist?

A critic of present political tendencies has remarked that "there is something rather pathetic in the vision of a Democracy demanding to be controlled by the state."[1] This critic presents himself as a defender of liberalism. His advice points to as near an approach to anarchy as is practically possible. Like that of the socialist, his counsel looks backward to laissez faire rather

[1] Brett, *A Defense of Liberty*.

than forward. His criticism, however, voices a common apprehension over the increasing burdens of the central government.

The socialist sees the trend towards centralization in government and the consequent tendency towards disruption of the established order. He rejoices in them. His liberal and conservative opponents see the same things and fear the advent of an efficient socialist bureaucracy built along the lines of the former German government or else the advent of an alternative tyranny of an inefficient type producing results comparable to the worst pictures of what the Bolsheviki did to Russia after the World War.

The socialist in his rejoicing and his opponents in their apprehension are alike in the one respect that they all think of government in terms of the past. Critics of socialism are correct in insisting that conflict of economic interests does not become any less significant with the failure of the market. They are correct also in their fears that a government adapted to the situation in which market control has prevailed cannot be depended upon to carry the burdens under which the market has broken down. They appear oblivious, however, to the prospect that current developments are moving towards such a reshaping of government organization as will rest it upon foundations quite different from those of an individualistic democracy. The present picture may not be one showing "Democracy demanding to be controlled by the state." Instead it may be one showing the traditional characters "Democracy" and "The State," as together victims of the cultural evolution juggernaut.

THE KINSHIP OF INSTITUTIONS

In such a discussion as this we need frequently to remind ourselves that the traditional separation of institutions into economic, political and other classes is only a method of abstraction hit upon for the sake of convenience and clearness of expression. The mere fact that the term political has been applied to some machinery of adjustment and the term economic to other institutional machinery does not destroy their kinship. To think otherwise is to make the mistake of the simple-minded student who wondered how the astronomers ever discovered the names of the stars.

The market rests upon the same fundamental grounds as the so-called political institutions which have accompanied it. In a broad sense the market is part of the machinery of government just as the principles which underlie the theory of market control are part of the prevailing system of law. Economic, political, governmental, legal and other institutions serving to effect adjustments of human interests, all develop out of a single process and together they constitute a coordinated unit. For this reason it is not particularly illuminating to say that current tendencies indicate a shifting of responsibilities from economic to governmental institutions. Governmental activities are becoming economic quite as truly as economic control is becoming governmental. In fact the economic organization has been in a broad sense governmental all along. The truth is that there is taking place in the fundamental cultural situation a change which involves a radical revision of all sorts of machinery of adjustment.

THE PROSPECTIVE ECONOMIC READJUSTMENT

It is a commonplace observation that human interests now run in terms which are in many respects different from those of a generation ago. The student of government is being compelled to talk in terms of such concepts as the pluralistic state. The economist must admit that economic issues run in somewhat altered terms. The individualistic analysis does not apply to current economic conflicts as neatly as it did to those of an earlier generation. The facts of increasing friction and unreconciled political and economic conflict between groups are patent. Continued increase of such friction and conflict would mean increasing disorganization and eventual disintegration of the cultural group from within or else its supplanting by less disorganized groups. Evidence of such imminent decay of Western civilization is not hard to find.[2] However, this evidence is more than offset by evidence of the essential strength of Western culture. The cornerstone of this strength, as heretofore indicated, lies in the prevalence of a common philosophical point of view and in the tremendous economic strength afforded by a highly developed technology. The strength of this twofold foundation furnishes the basis for a prediction that an adjustment will be effected between disruptive political and economic interests which are now unreconciled.

[2] *Cf.* Spengler, *Untergang des Abend-landes.*

ECONOMIC READJUSTMENT

Social reorganization means the development of processes of adjustment to which members of the social group give a common support. This is not possible so long as large classes in the group are antagonistic to prevailing machinery of adjustment.

The development of a common allegiance does not, of course, depend upon an equally active participation in the processes of social control by all members or all classes of the group. The prospect of a stable economic régime, coupled with the modern concentration of wealth, has suggested the possibility of an aristocracy of wealth motivated by a spirit of *noblesse oblige*. However, such a development appears altogether unlikely. The traditional inheritance which has come down to typically Western peoples out of a laissez faire period is quite antagonistic to such a development. A much more reasonable expectation is that processes of adjustment will be developed through which conflicting interests will serve to check each other. The market régime constituted such a system as long as its operation afforded results which appealed to the bulk of the members of the cultural group as equitable. It does not now produce such results. It does not have that universal respect which is requisite to effective social cooperation.

It is a mistake to emphasize the market as the essential feature of the laissez faire period. The market was the focal point of economic institutional organization. It was the form in which a principle became effective. The fundamental principle of the system was the regulation and control of conflicting interests through a mutual checking and restraint. When we say that our economic organization has ceased to be competitive, the statement means that conflicting interests do not now check and regulate each other in an efficient, economical manner. To defend the market blindly now as a fundamental basis of economic organization is to forsake a principle for an outgrown form—a sin common to many peoples and many generations. If the formal machinery of competition is retained now through social inertia, after it has ceased to be the means of application of the principle which originally it represented, then its retention is indeed such a "tyranny of the machine" as is claimed by socialists. Enforced retention of the machine by an interested class would be a tyranny of that class however benevolent its intentions and actions might be.

In summary then, an economic readjustment can be counted upon to consist of a revision of institutional machinery rather than a forsaking of the principle of control through conflict. Whatever the precise form of machinery developed we can expect a mutual restraint and control of conflicting interests. And, in any case, the analogy between physical laws and economic laws will be as valid as it has ever been. Conflicting interests may be expected to run in terms different from those of an individualistic laissez faire régime, but that is a fact so patent that it is of only incidental significance.

NEED FOR RECONSTRUCTION OF THEORY

The confusion and disappearance of traditional lines between different classes of institutions is evidence that a process of reconstruction of institutions is going forward. That we cannot take the evidence at hand and tell more about the process is to be attributed, in large measure, to the fact that men have not been in the habit of thinking about social phenomena in consistently objective terms. In economics, the dominant system of theory has tended to remain static. The rigidity of the system has often been made the basis for calling economics a science. Undoubtedly this rigidity has done much to give the subject an established place among the different branches of learning. And undoubtedly through its rigidity the system has been practically useful in the solution of many economic problems.[3] In an essentially competitive organization it has served both as an explanation of phenomena and as an ideal of social organization. But the self-sufficiency and rigidity of the system are effective barriers to its development.

The history of economic institutions and the history of economic theories show a much more closely connected continuity in the development of institutions. The institutions of one generation tend to grow gradually into those of a following generation. They fall far short of a lineal descent but nevertheless show more continuity than succeeding systems of theory. Fundamental systems of social theory do not develop directly from one to another.[4] Each is built up from the prevailing system

[3] Wesley C. Mitchell, Introduction to *The Trend of Economics*, edited by R. J. Tugwell.

[4] Minor variations and offshoots from a system of theory do frequently develop directly from a parent system. For example the economic theory of Marx shows its descent from Ricardo. But

of institutions rather than from a preceding system of theory. Such, at least, has been the case in the past and is the present necessity. Whether it will continue to be so need not concern us here.

Those who undertake to formulate a system of economic theory based primarily upon the objective point of view must expect unfavorable comparison of their tentative formulations with the system of competitive theory. They must expect also the contrast of their efforts with work done in the more favorably situated physical and biological sciences. But criticism and unfavorable comparisons do not detract from the significance of such efforts. Work from an objective point of view ought at least to afford a more consistently effective cumulative accomplishment than has been characteristic of contributions to competitive economic theory.

ACCOUNTS AND INSTITUTIONAL RECONSTRUCTION

Greatly increased importance is now being given to accounts by both economic and political developments. When the market was typically the effective arbiter of

such variations do not represent fundamentally new systems. The development of a system of theory describing an economic organization which is one aspect of a general cultural reorganization is not to be arrived at by a rational reformulation of old dogma which applied to an earlier and essentially different situation.

Speaking of the relation of quantitative investigation to orthodox economic theory Wesley C. Mitchell aptly says, "There is little likelihood that the old explanations will be refuted by these investigators, but much likelihood that they will be disregarded." "Quantitative Analysis in Economic Theory," *American Economic Review*, March 1925.

economic conflicts, accounting was wholly subordinate to it.[5] Accounting meant giving double entry bookkeeping expression to legal and market relationships. Accounting theory, what there was of it, was as subordinate to law as it was to the market. Accounting had no independent standing. But as economic activities and economic organization have developed since the industrial revolution, direct control by the market has become incapable of adjusting new forms of conflicting interests. The functions of accounting have expanded to cover the adjustment of many interests not directly adjusted by the market. The theory of accounts has acquired an independent status. The extent to which this independent standing of accounts has developed is indicated by the fact of an increasing readiness of ·courts of law to give heed to accounting principles and to adjust legal rules thereto.

When the market has failed to regulate certain economic activities effectively, the government has stepped in to assume a direct responsibility for them. This change has been of very great importance in the development of an independent status of accounts. In their early history, regulating commissions were somewhat at sea. They could not turn to the market for the market had failed to meet the situation. They owed their existence to its failure. When they turned to the law they found it assuming an adjustment of economic interests accord-

[5] It must be remembered always that the market is now a more highly perfected tool than it has ever been before. Its decreasing effectiveness is not due to its internal deterioration but to its changing environment. *Cf.* p. 36.

ing to the principles of a competitive régime. As a result, instead of depending upon the market or upon law, regulating commissions turned to accounts and accounting principles for guidance and support. Such a result was not intended by those who initiated government regulation. It was intended that regulation should be a further agency for the enforcement of the old law of the competitive or individualistic situation. But the effect of regulation has been the formulation of new law rather than a mere enforcement of the old. And because commissions have been dependent upon accounting principles to guide their decisions, accounting has been the major source of the new law developed by regulation.[6]

The resort to accounts as a source of the administrative law of government regulation; the recognition of accounting principles in the application of more general rules of law by courts of law, and the increasing importance of accounts to private business management are all parts of a single pattern. Whether business is public, semi-public or private, it has come to hinge upon accounts. The most significant thing in current institutional development relative to the adjustment of economic interests is not a shifting of responsibility from economic to governmental machinery. It is rather a shifting of responsibility to accounting processes of adjustment and an organization of economic control about accounts.[7] So

[6] See note 3, p. 170.
[7] *Cf.* "Social Control Through Accounts," by C. Rufus Rorem in the *Accounting Review* for September 1928. Also the same writer's *Accounting Method*, Chs. 1, 2 and 40.

pervasive is this tendency that it promises a leading rôle for accounts in the process of institutional reconstruction. Indeed, circumstantial evidence points to the conclusion that just as market machinery and the principles involved in market control were absorbed into the government and law of an individualistic period, so accounting technique and accounting theory are destined to be absorbed into the government and law of a succeeding period.

RELATIONS OF ACCOUNTS AND STATISTICS

It is perhaps desirable to return at this time to some points made in the previous chapter. It has been stated that accounting technique and accounting theory are themselves in process of development. Accounts are tending, in a narrow sense, to become an application of statistical methods to the problems of business control. In a broader sense, they are becoming the application of statistical methods to the adjustment of conflicting economic interests. A situation has arisen in which it is impossible to draw rigid lines of distinction between accounting principles and legal principles or between market control and accounting control. This incorporation of accounting technique into prevailing processes of adjustment is a step in the fulfillment of the foregoing definition of accounts. Thus the absorption of accounts into law and government already has taken place to a considerable degree. To that extent the foregoing analogy between the market and accounts is a matter of historical record rather than a prophecy of future development.

Attention has been called to the place of statistical methods in the progress which the objective point of view is making in a development of the social sciences.[8] The conclusion has been drawn that in the course of time man will acquire a control over his social environment comparable to his present control over his physical environment. Or, putting the case more accurately, the actions of men in relation to social phenomena will come to be controlled in a way comparable to present control over their actions relative to physical phenomena. If this is indeed an accurate diagnosis, then statistical technique is of transcendent importance. It not only represents a means of progress by the social sciences but is at the same time a pivotal instrument of social evolution and social control.

In the light of this appraisal of statistical technique, the current tendency in accounts takes on an added significance. The dominance of statistics in accounts is only one phase of the general rôle now being played by statistics. The conclusion is suggested that economic organization around accounts is merely the economic aspect of a cultural reorganization upon the basis of an objective point of view. Accounting and statistical methods are rigidly confined to the use of objective terms.[9] Hence their usefulness as instruments in this particular cultural reorganization.

[8] *Cf.* Ch. VII.
[9] *Cf.* J. Rufus Rorem, "Similarities of Accounting and Statistical Method," *Accounting Review*, March 1927.

THE ACCOUNTING PROFESSION

The rise of accounts to importance has bestowed upon the accountant a professional status. He is not yet received into full fellowship by the older professions but that is somewhat like social recognition. It will come in the course of time. His responsibilities to his clients and to the public have been clearly developed. If now, in truth, accounts are to be the hub for an economic reorganization will not the significance of the accounting profession be still further enhanced? Will that responsibility which the market has failed to carry find its new resting place in the accounting profession? Do we, after all, look forward to a personal or professional arbitration of economic interests—a bureaucracy of the accountants?

If this were a novel and the accountant were our hero, such doubtless would be a fitting *dénouement*. But as a solution of the current problem of economic control it is not in the least probable. German and Russian experiences afford some of the nearest modern approaches to a bureaucracy of officials. Anglo-Saxon tradition is contrary to it. The notion that an official is only a citizen representing other citizens is too deeply seated to give way easily. Unification of so-called Anglo-Saxon peoples upon the basis of an official bureaucracy is scarcely more plausible than their unification upon the basis of an aristocracy of wealth. Furthermore there is in the work of the accounting profession itself, evidence that accountants will not become such a bureaucracy. The accountant enjoys no special claim upon the confidence of opposing economic groups. The nature of his work is tending to make him more of a protagonist rather than less so. He frequently serves as the confidential advisor of business executives. In legal disputes involving large sums, prominent accounting firms are apt to be employed to supplement the work of legal counsel. This phase of the development of accounting practice makes it all the more unlikely that accountants will be called upon to carry any special responsibility for the administration of a coming economic régime. Undoubtedly the accountng profession will continue to hold a position of importance but it is hardly destined to be an Atlas and carry an economic world upon its shoulders.

ACCOUNTING THEORY VS. COMPETITIVE ECONOMIC THEORY

Opposing schools of economic thought and individual critics have assailed competitive economic theory upon many different grounds. Proponents of the system, in their less exasperated moments, have rejoined calmly, "All right, give us something better."

How good is the theory of economic organization around the competitive market? Is it a satisfactory summary or explanation of current economic affairs?

If the current situation shows a constant drift away from market control, then competitive theory is becoming less and less satisfactory. We may not be able to set a valuation upon it but at least we can tell in an objective way the change which is coming in the rôle which it plays in social organization. Furthermore, if the current situation discloses a drift towards some other form of organization, a basis should thereby be afforded for prediction with reference to a "better" system of theory. If accounts are supplanting the market as a focal point of *de facto* economic organization it is reasonable to expect that accounting theory should supplant market theory and so become the "better" system. Is there any evidence that such a substitution is taking place or is likely to take place?

It might well be pleaded that even if accounting control supplants market control, it is not to be expected that a theory of accounting control should be developed contemporaneously with the fact of accounting control. The theory of market control developed much later than the fact of market control. Hence it might well be concluded that as yet we can not undertake to discuss the development of a theory of accounting control even granting that from an institutional standpoint accounting control is becoming a fact. Nevertheless, there are some things which can be said now relative to the possible development of such a system of theory.

In the first place it may be pointed out that the above suggestion does not require a literal substitution of existing accounting theory for current theory of market control. Accounting theory obviously is not now a general theory of economic control. The present suggestion is that if accounts should supplant the market as the focal point of economic organization, then a new theory of economic control should take its rise out of existing accounting theory. This suggestion is quite in keeping with the

242 GOVERNMENT, ACCOUNTS, MARKET

hypothesis that a new system of theory must come from the concrete institutional situation for that is precisely the source of accounting principles. The development of accounting theory is under the direct and constant influence of the actual conflict of economic interests.[10]

In the second place it is pertinent to point out how, through its failure to develop, the theory of competitive organization is failing to account for current economic phenomena satisfactorily. Such a system of theory does not start from existing economic phenomena and arrive at the competitive analysis as the best available explanation of the observed facts. That was the way in which the system originated but in modern discussions of the theory of a competitive system the procedure is to start with an assumption of competition upon which an abstract system is built. Allowances are then made to adjust the system, piecemeal, to actual situations. A perfect fit, so the argument runs, is not to be expected any more than we can expect to find the different laws of physics independently exemplified in natural phenomena. "Of course we assume competition!" This exclamation was that of an economist whose viewpoint is that of prevailing competitive theory. It was expressed in the course of a discussion with the writer. He continued, "You cannot build up a system or do any effective think-

[10] It may well be pointed out here that if a new system of theory develops, as here suggested, the relation of its origin to the statistical method will be no less significant than its relation to accounts. In fact its dependence upon the statistical method must be the broader and more general conception.

ACCOUNTING VS. ECONOMIC THEORY

ing upon the basis of an assumption of general monopoly."

Note the begging of the question involved in this statement! The alternative to control by competition is still an organization around the market, albeit a moribund one in which monopoly has taken the place of competition. But the actual economic organization of society does not remain static. Organization around the market is not to be assumed as a necessary basis of economic cooperation.

As implied above, the development of competitive theory has not been confined to summary descriptions of the operation of markets. Economic theorists of the utility, pain cost and utility *vs.* pain cost schools have busied themselves more with the task of setting up a system of values which is supposed to underlie and explain the operations of actual markets. This system of values purports to have translated the phenomena of the actual market into terms of human nature on the one hand and a natural environment on the other hand. But when the effort is actually made to tie up this system of subjective formulations with actual market phenomena the best that is achieved is a sort of parallelism in which the subjective formulations have no meaning except as they are related to and directly dependent upon the objective phenomena of the market.[11] Proof of the equivalence of utilities is found solely in the actions of individuals. When it is observed that interest rates persist in actual markets with a considerable degree of constancy it is concluded that

[11] *Cf.* Wicksteed, *Common Sense of Political Economy*, p. 76.

the explanation is in "The persistent traits of human psychology—an enduring and apparently fairly constant element of human nature."[12] Terms like "rate of impatience" and "time preference" are set up by "psychological theorists" to explain the interest phenomenon.

It is to be noted that in such reasoning as is involved in the above expressions, argument runs from the market to human nature rather than the other way around. And so it is with all utility theory. Economic theory has not explained the market in terms of human nature and a natural environment. In fact there can be no valid contrast between nature and human nature. A fundamental analysis of economic phenomena must run in other terms. As has been stated at an earlier point in this discussion, progress in the social sciences is to be made by keeping the individual within the scope of causal relationships. Any explanation of economic phenomena purporting to run in terms of an independent human nature is no explanation as long as that human nature is not independently determined.

Since the theory of a competitive system assumes competition it does not apply to a situation in which the competitive market does not fit. Nor does such a system of theory become any more generally applicable by resting it upon a human nature which has been constructed on the basis of familiar market phenomena. As the cultural situation has changed from that which gave rise to organization around the market, the contrast between the abstract system of competitive economic theory and the

[12] Ely *et al.*, *Outlines of Economics*, 4th Ed., p. 510.

actual operation of the market has been emphasized. In accounting for the increasing rift between prevailing theory and current facts a continually larger and larger allowance for practical complications has become necessary. Unsolved economic problems, that is, unadjusted economic conflicts, have forced upon the economist an alternative similar to that which has confronted jurists in their treatment of exceptional cases at law. The individualistic system of law has suffered no matter which of the alternatives presented has been accepted by the courts in their treatment of exceptional cases. And so competitive economic theory loses, no matter which horn of his dilemma is accepted by the economist in his treatment of exceptional economic problems. Thus the economist is compelled to face the question of the adequacy of competitive theory.

Some have argued that competitive theory is generally applicable to current economic situations such as that in the United States and that although the fit may not be perfect there never has been a time or situation in which it was more nearly perfect. Others have argued that competitive theory is a product of historical development; that it is an outgrowth of a particular cultural situation and that with a different situation such as now is in process of development it must give way to a different system of theory. The reader will appreciate that the latter view is assumed in this discussion.

One may, in form at least, avoid taking sides in this issue as to the goodness of competitive theory. The authors of one of the current widely used economic textbooks have done so by using competitive theory when it has seemed desirable to them to do so without committing themselves for or against it. They have "tried to avoid any artificial separation of 'theory' and 'practical problems.'"[13] In adhering to this purpose they have avoided the formulation of a systematic or rigid body of theory. Their emphasis has been placed upon an introduction of the student to reasonable interpretations of current economic phenomena. Their procedure in this respect is somewhat parallel to that of administrators of the law when their attention has been given to the effecting of practical adjustments to the exclusion of the preservation of a social ideal.[14]

Although the authors of the above mentioned text have refrained from taking sides for or against competitive theory, and this position of neutrality may truly represent their several attitudes, nevertheless their method constitutes a defection from active support of competitive theory. Their disregard is more insidious and is perhaps more destructive than an unsympathetic frontal attack would be; a boring from within, so to speak.

Turning again to accounting theory we may well raise the question of the trend in its development in order to see if it affords any promise of becoming a theory of economic organization.

The substitution of an accrual basis for the cash basis in a determination of incomes and expenses for a given fiscal period is a change which has definitely taken place

[13] Ely *et al.*, *Outlines of Economics*. *Cf.* Preface to 4th Ed.
[14] *Cf.* Ch. XI.

in accounting theory. It has come to be accepted even in the legal application of accounting rules.[15] Nevertheless no satisfactory theory of accruals has been developed. Accountants, for example, are not agreed as to the propriety of applying the accrual basis to necessary periodic costs of idle capacity in manufacturing and transportation. A plant which is built to carry a peak load cannot be fully utilized at other times. Facilities provided to handle the large volume of output when production is at a maximum must be carried through periods when production is at a minimum. Whether such costs of idle capacity should be charged against the period when they must be met or should be allocated to periods of large production is one upon which accountants are not agreed. This divergence of presumably authoritative opinions is due to unforeseen difficulties involved in the adoption of an accrual basis.

Only such incomes and expenses as are directly related to each other are to be included in the income or operating statement for a given fiscal period. No rule of thumb like the receipt and disbursement of cash is adequate to determine which incomes and expenses are to be selected for inclusion in the statement. It may be said that the expenses of a given fiscal period are the costs of obtaining the incomes of that period. But this statement can not be turned around to read also that the incomes of a given period are those arising as a result of the expenses of the period. Whether a given income is to be included

[15] Note that this is legal application of accounting rules not accounting application of legal rules.

among those of a given fiscal period depends upon the effect of its inclusion upon the claims of the parties at interest in the accounting adjustment.[16] In practice different rules or principles have developed with respect to accrual of different kinds of incomes and expenses. The consolidation of these different rules into a comprehensive, consistent theory of accruals must go back to the compromise and adjustment of the different interests at stake in the accounting record. Thus the adoption of an accrual basis for the allocation of incomes and expenses has raised an accounting problem which is as yet unsolved but which is as broad in its scope as the market adjustment of conflicting economic interests. A satisfactory solution of this accounting problem may well afford a theory of accounting control which is as general in its application as the theory of market control.[17]

The compromise of conflicting interests is a process of valuation. It accomplishes social organization and results in a distribution of economic incomes. Value and distribution constitute a single problem and accounting theory is especially and peculiarly a treatment of that problem. Accounting theory deals with problems of value and distribution in their current concrete forms. Market

[16] *Cf.* the writer's *Theory of Accounts*, Vol. I, p. 57.

[17] The suggestion has been advanced that the fundamental outcome of accounting control will be to fasten the norms and forms of competition more firmly upon economic organization and so to perpetuate control by the market. However, such an hypothesis assumes a static character in accounts. It is wholly inconsistent with the evolution which is actually taking place in accounting technique and theory.

theory deals with them in forms which were typical of an earlier economic period. Thus there is some evidence in the current development of accounting theory itself that it is, logically, heir apparent to the position now occupied by market theory.

MITCHELL'S WORK ON CYCLES

Not even a passing reference to current theoretical developments can omit mention of such studies of economic mechanism as those of Prof. Wesley C. Mitchell in the field of business cycles.

In his discussion of the business cycle Professor Mitchell builds upon the conception of economic organization through competitive business enterprise. Thus his initial postulate agrees with that of so-called static economics. But in his method Professor Mitchell departs from precedents established by economists whose work runs in static terms. His procedure, with its objective emphasis, is in a measure a return to the method of common sense observation appealed to so frequently by Adam Smith. Smith's use of such a viewpoint aided in the formulation of a body of static theory. It is pertinent to our discussion at this point to speculate as to what will be the outcome of using a similar method in the existing situation.

Professor Mitchell has presented the goal of his work on cycles as a comprehensive analytical description of the phenomenon with sufficient synthesis to bring it out from behind the screen of detailed variations which clothes each actual cycle. In this connection we may repeat a quotation from him as follows:

"The cycles with which the discussion will deal are neither the cycles of history nor the cycles of some speculative construction, but cycles of an intermediate order." [18]

Suppose that through such a combination of analysis and synthesis Professor Mitchell is able to arrive at an adequate mechanistic explanation of the business cycle, what will be the significance of his accomplishment for the general theory of economic organization?

Possibly Professor Mitchell would insist that the task of accounting for the business cycle is complex enough by itself without dragging in the question of economic organization in general. However, he cannot be allowed to escape the issue here raised on grounds of modesty. Surely an adequate discussion of the cycles problem includes its relation to the general problem of economic organization!

When economists developed the theory of economic organization around the market, the formulation of that theory fostered a further development of such a form of organization in practice. The competitive system became a norm or ideal of economic organization just as democracy became an ideal of political organization. If, now, Professor Mitchell's "cycles of an intermediate order" lead to an adequate explanation of the cycle phenomenon what will be the effect of that explanation upon the cycles of actual affairs? Will they tend to conform to the normal or ideal cycle? Surely not! Survival value lies not in the cycle but in avoidance of it. One might just as

[18] *Business Cycles, The Problem and Its Setting*, p. 469.

well expect an adequate explanation of yellow fever to result in a general indulgence in the disease.

When Professor Mitchell's "cycles of an intermediate order," or their progeny and other influences, so control the management of business enterprise that cycles become as extinct as yellow fever epidemics now are, then what will be the accepted theory of economic organization?

Professor Mitchell has, upon more than one occasion, made it clear that he does not expect objective investigation to afford mere inductive verification of the accepted doctrines of static theory.[19] And this position is all right as far as it goes. However, as a declaration of faith on his part, it does not go far enough. Does he expect the body of doctrine to be afforded by objective study to be better than orthodox static theory as an interpretation of the economic phenomena of England and the United States in the seventeenth, eighteenth and nineteenth centuries? Or does he hold that the new theory will both run in terms of different concepts and typify a different order of facts?

Very properly Professor Mitchell makes business profits the starting point of his discussion of the business cycle. This is inevitable because the business cycle is a product of the competitive market situation. But does he expect the rôle of business profits, as the chief factor in economic control, to long survive under changing

[19] *Cf.* his presidential address before the American Economic Association, *American Economic Review*, March 1925.

economic conditions? Will not his own objective analysis help to modify fundamentally the rôle of profits?

If a recasting of economic organization were dependent primarily upon the successful prosecution of such studies as Professor Mitchell has laid out for himself, this speculation would be as far fetched as it may now appear to the most skeptical of readers. But in truth the current economic reorganization is no more dependent upon such studies than the establishment of the modern market system was dependent upon Smith's writing *The Wealth of Nations*.

THE RÔLE OF BUSINESS PROFITS

The concept of business profits calls to mind the merchant adventurer who set out upon perilous voyages trusting to a kindly Providence and to his own adventurous spirit to bring him home safely with a handsome profit. The later developed business venture of production for the market was a direct successor to such trading expeditions of the merchant adventurer. The analogy between the two was very close in the early history of the modern market régime. The competitive market system became established through the activities of enterprisers who took the initiative in assuming responsibilities and risks involved in their control of production and exchange. A relatively free initiative attained the dignity of an economic order because it worked well and it worked well because it was suited to control of the relatively simple economic processes of the time. The system arose under a régime of handicraft technology. In such a

THE RÔLE OF BUSINESS PROFITS 253

technology there was no complicated interrelation of processes such as characterizes machine production. Assembling the prerequisites to production did not require much technical organization, or time, or a large investment of capital. A free for all competition between entrepreneurs eliminated the incompetent through their failure and left economic administration in the hands of the more efficient. This great social advantage was achieved at relatively little social cost on account of the character of the processes of production and exchange. Failure of the incompetent meant relatively much gain and little loss. Even the failure of a merchant with large investments in ships and consumption goods carried with it no serious social loss.

The present economic situation, however, is quite different from that which prevailed in the earlier history of the competitive régime. Through technological developments the processes of production have become minutely interdependent. The investment in productive equipment has grown to enormous proportions. Modern economic organization for production and exchange has become a vast, complex and sensitive mechanism. Furthermore, the competitive régime has developed an increasing tendency for incompetent entrepreneurs to fail *en masse* rather than individually, with the result that they frequently have dragged down with them many who were not particularly incompetent. The situation has become such that society can no longer afford to give free scope to the enterprise of the old-time merchant adventurer even in his modified rôle of production for profit. Productive and distributive processes can no longer be entrusted to the keeping of good, bad and indifferent entrepreneur managers who are engaged in a free for all struggle for control of them. The old-fashioned entrepreneur fits into the current economic situation like the proverbial bull in a china shop.

Something of the current trend in management was suggested in Chapter VIII of this discussion. The adjustment of management to a new environment is being worked out primarily by those engaged in management just as was the case in the establishment of the competitive market régime. Even in a corporate enterprise of the sort that is still subject to one-man control, the manager who pointed with pride to large past profits, and spoke in glowing generalities of future prospects, is being supplanted. The new manager is one who speaks with increasing assurance of next year's profits. Management has come to run in terms of a much longer time perspective. On account of this fact, and the conditions which have given rise to it, management is developing into a form of control which is exercised by an organized group of executives in the place of control by a single individual. In such an organization, trial by bankruptcy can not be applied separately to the different executives. Other means must be resorted to for measurement of their individual efficiency. And since the management can be and is replaced piece-meal the bankruptcy test is no longer applicable even for maintenance of the efficiency of the executive organization as a whole. As the processes to be controlled have changed, management also has changed. The processes of production and transportation of goods have become so highly technical and interdependent that continued dependence upon the profits test to maintain efficiency of administration would be, from the group point of view, a suicidal policy.

Modern developments in management are reflected in the principles and policies of accounting. When we turn to accounts for their version of entrepreneur profits we find them ignoring the concept altogether. Corporate management has developed a settled policy of fixing a dividend rate which can be maintained regardless of the net income for the particular period. Extraordinary gains and losses are ruled out of the income account. They have become mere surplus adjustments. Comparableness of the net income item for different periods is an essential dogma of accounting. The elimination of extraordinary influences, including the effects of changes in the price level, and a constant improvement in methods of allocating costs are aiding very greatly towards increasing the trustworthiness of the net income item and in making it more nearly comparable for different periods. By a process of elimination of disturbing causes, net income is left as a resultant from the ordinary predictable processes of the business enterprise in question.

As management develops more fully its time perspective, it increases both its control over factors within the scope of its administration and its power of adjustment to conditions which it cannot control. This increased power of adjustment on the part of the business unit has an obvious survival value. However, from the social point of view, a more important consideration is the fact that it tends to eliminate economic friction and waste.

Management from a long run viewpoint eliminates waste and friction both through more efficient administration while it is in control and through increased avoidance of the social loss incident to bankruptcy. This elimination of friction makes for stability. Economic stability increases the assurance with which management can chart its future course, thus increasing its efficiency and bringing about a further elimination of maladjustments. The effect is, therefore, cumulative.

In the earlier course of this discussion grounds were advanced for believing that a period of economic stability lies ahead. That stability is not a far-off shadowy event. It is even now emerging through the good offices of an evolving business management.

In a cultural organization characterized by a maximum control over man's action by his knowledge of his physical and social environments, effective prediction in economic affairs must become the rule rather than the exception. Of course prediction in human affairs cannot become perfect as long as the riddle of human experience remains unsolved. And there is no reason at all to suppose that a mere cultural reorganization will solve that enduring puzzle. However, it is quite plausible that prediction should be developed to such a point that an assumption of foreknowledge may become a general basis for social organization. Such an assumption bids fair to become as typical of the concrete facts of actual economic processes as were the assumptions of individualistic static economics in relation to the facts of an earlier situation to which they were applied. For example, effective prediction may become as general and as typical as the mobility of factors of production ever was.

The concept of business profits presupposes a situation in which the entrepreneur manager steers the business enterprise upon a relatively uncharted course. A general acceptance of the market system represented an agreement in advance as to the manner of division of the undetermined proceeds of such enterprises. But, in practice, business management has become a matter of navigating a fully charted course with the aid of so many safety devices and such effective technique that even the details of the voyage can be foreseen with a constantly increasing accuracy. In this latter situation the problem of dividing the proceeds—that is the distribution of the economic dividend—becomes quite a different problem. And no amount of indirection on the part of the law and professional economists can so turn back the clock that it will be the same problem. Custom and law tend to enforce adjustments in terms of traditional processes, while the changed form of the problem demands a new solution.

The current economic situation affords an abundance of illustrations of the continued effective operation of the traditional economic organization. By concentrating his attention upon those aspects of the situation in which traditional doctrines are exemplified, the defender of orthodox, static theory easily convinces himself that the fundamental economic situation has not changed. For him exceptions to the traditional rules are still exceptions.

But to the man who concentrates his attention upon unquestioned changes, and studies trends in concrete phenomena, the current situation appears in an altogether different light. For him exceptions to the traditional rules have themselves become the rule. To him a preponderance of economic facts appear as unruly sheep which have broken out of the traditional fold. He seeks a new fold in which they can be corralled; a fold which in time will include also the meeker members of the flock still remaining in the familiar fold.

As long as defenders and critics of any system of economic theory concentrate their attention upon different aspects of the multitude of economic facts, they obviously cannot reach an agreement. When the exasperated economic theorist says to his pestiferous, unorthodox critics, "Well, suppose you give us something better," the best available answer of those critics is, perhaps, "Wait and see." That, at least, is the answer to which the present discussion leads.

CRITICISM BY THE LATE PROFESSOR YOUNG

In criticism of the hypothesis that accounts are destined to supplant the market as a focal point of economic organization, the late Prof. Allyn A. Young made the following statement:

"Accounting, as I see it, is no possible substitute for the market because accounting cannot supply, of itself, any criteria of control. At present, I repeat, accounting gets its *concepts* from the market. Its aim is to portray the position of the individual undertaking in a general market situation. Conceivably what you call market control may be replaced by some other type of control, and a new type of control would call for a new type of accounting concepts. But the essence of the new system would be found, not in its tool, accounting, but in the norms which accounting would utilize." [20]

This statement deserves careful consideration.

It might well be argued that the essence of the competitive system is to be found, not in its tool, the market, but in the norms or ideals which are given effect through the market.

In earlier chapters of this discussion it has been argued that the modern market has developed as part of a larger cultural mechanism. The principles of competitive control have served to guide economic conduct and to coordinate it with conduct in other aspects of a larger social situation. It has been argued further that a new cultural mechanism is now developing and that its development must bring with it a new economic mechanism and new criteria of economic conduct. If this diagnosis is to be accepted, the new economic mechanism and the new criteria of economic conduct must develop out of the existing economic situation. A continuity of the *de facto* economic organization of the group is indispensable to group survival. But at the same time such a new economic mechanism and such new criteria must be coordinated parts of the new general social organization. That is, they must tie in with both the transition situation and the basic foundation of the new organization.

[20] Quoted from criticisms written privately to the writer.

Accounting technique has become an indispensable feature of current economic organization. The modern business enterprise is no more free from the necessity of using accounts than it would be free from market control in a competitive situation. The development of adequate rules governing the use of accounts and an accurate observation of these rules have, therefore, become indispensable conditions of group welfare. The public interest has now come to require the general observance of correct accounting principles just as it once demanded that the market be kept open and free.[21]

In the fundamental argument of this volume there is the suggestion that the principles of accounting adjustment are destined to become a closer approximation of the principles or "laws" of physical science than has ever been achieved by the principles or "laws" of competitive economic control. This suggestion is not supported merely by the increasing importance of the rôle played by accounts in economic organization. It is sustained also by the fact that accounts tie in with the statistical method and the scientific movement or objective viewpoint which are held herein to be immediately dominant factors in the shaping of a new cultural organization. Accounts thus fulfill the twofold qualification laid down above for a new economic mechanism. That is, they are related in a functional way with both the existing economic situation and the prospective cultural organization. Their relation to the actual situation is sufficiently indicated when we point out that accounts are indispensable

[21] *Cf.* pp. 38 and 187 above.

in the current economic organization and have developed out of practical affairs just as the common law developed. Their relation to the prospective cultural organization is through their relation to the statistical method. This relationship is indicated in our definition of accounting as the application of statistical methods to problems of economic control.[22] It is expressed again in the suggestion that economic reorganization around accounting technique is but the representation in a limited field of a general social reorganization which is being worked out through the utilization of statistical methods.

The market and accounts can both be interpreted in either subjective or mechanistic terms. The adjustment of conflicting individual interests through mutual restraint and control has long been a social ideal. The market is a tool or means of giving effect to that ideal in respect to economic adjustments. Other means give effect to the same ideal in other respects, as for example in legal adjustments.

The market form of adjustment may also become a tool of particular business interests. Every promoter of city subdivisions who organizes an auction sale of lots thereby sets up market machinery to serve his own particular ends. In this case, clearly, the process of market adjustment is open to both subjective and objective interpretation.

It must be admitted that in a thoroughgoing competitive system, accounting is subordinate to the market. This, however, does not mean that in the existing situ-

[22] *Cf.* p. 218.

ation accounting is entirely dependent upon the market. It is not. The market does not distinguish between surplus adjustments and revenue items in accounts, nor does it afford the basis for income and expense accruals. Accounting does not accept the market's concept of entrepreneur profits. In fact, the accounting concept of profits, like many other accounting concepts, is a direct outcome of the appearance in the market of cooperative forms of enterprise like the corporation. Other concepts, like that of continuous accounting control, have resulted from the use of machine technology. Indeed, concepts which are not essentially products of the market constitute a very considerable part of accounting theory. Accounting concepts come out of the actual conflict of economic interests. That is a reason why they must be entirely subordinate to the market in a thoroughly competitive situation.

It is true that double entry bookkeeping originated as a device for recording market adjustments. Accounting technique still serves that end, but at the same time it does much more than that. And, as the functions of accounting technique have increased, an increasing number of rules or principles have been developed to govern its uses. These rules, or standards of practice, have developed as supplementary to market control rather than as subordinate to it. They are criteria of economic conduct just as truly as are the "laws" of competition. That they do not yet constitute a group or social ideal is assumed in the present argument which is devoted partly to reasons why they may be expected to develop into such an ideal. The fact that they have not yet done so is no proof that they will not become a unified system of criteria interpreting a new economic situation.

In the present state of our knowledge of social phenomena, such a prediction cannot be supported in matter-of-fact terms like the dicta of physical science. Hence the reader is compelled to choose between the tentative evidence and suggestions here presented and the disbelief expressed by Professor Young.

SUMMARY

1. Current tendencies show a rapid increase of burdens thrust upon central governments. Opponents of this trend view it with apprehension because they consider government incapable of bearing the burdens under which the market has broken down.

2. This apprehension is correct as applied to the governments of an individualistic period. But a different cultural situation is shaping a new scheme of institutions including those of government and politics.

3. The basic principle of the so-called competitive system was a mutual checking and control of conflicting interests. The fundamental economic problem of the current transition period is to perpetuate this principle rather than to preserve or to reestablish the competitive market. The market was only a form of economic organization through which this principle found expression. The fundamental principle of adjustment through conflict and mutual restraint is not to be identified with the market system.

4. In the development of government regulation, accounting has been a fruitful source of new administrative law. Indeed, the outstanding economic tendency of the present time is not so much a shifting of responsibility to political institutions as it is an increasing dependence upon accounts. There is prospect that accounts and accounting theory will be absorbed into government and law in the same sense that the market and market theory were in an earlier period.

5. Economic organization around accounts may be interpreted as the economic aspect of a cultural organization upon the basis of an objective viewpoint.

6. Accounting and statistical methods are serving as vehicles of the current cultural reorganization because of their characteristic limitation of expression to objective terms.

7. If accounts are to supplant the market as the chief basis of economic organization, it is reasonable to expect that accounting theory should supplant market theory as the summary theoretical interpretation of contemporary economic phenomena.

8. But granting that accounting control is becoming institutionally a fact, a systematic theory of accounting control can be expected to make its appearance only at a somewhat later date. However, in the adoption of an accrual basis for income and expense determination, accountants have raised a problem which can be dealt with satisfactorily only upon the basis of principles which are as broad in their application to current economic problems as the theory of market control has ever been.

CHAPTER XV

THE FUTURE OF ECONOMIC CONTROL

Economic control in the past, that is in our own modern past, has been essentially laissez faire or competitive control. At the present time it is a mixture of controls by many different agencies. The market still occupies a position of authority without being authoritative. Its position has been likened to that of a monarch who has lost the loyal support of his subjects. Perhaps a better figure of speech would be to say that it is an idol of the tribe—particularly of the Anglo-Saxon tribe.

Many of us in the tribe have come to do this idol lip service only. But like all superstitious tribesmen we are not quite sure that dire results would not follow if we actually toppled the old idol from his pedestal. He may be only a poor idol but we demand the protection of a better tribal god before we turn our faces away from him.

There is something childish and helpless in this demand for a better tribal god. Better idols of the tribe are to be had by working for them, not for the asking. For those who are still so under the sway of the old idol that they fear the passing of our economic system from a competitive régime, it should be reassuring that we already have made the passage safely. It is one of the purposes of this chapter to show how the passage has come about.

The passing of our economic system from a régime of

competitive control means an actual though not necessarily a formal dethronement of the market. In Chapter IV we considered various factors tending to undermine market control. The business cycle was cited as the chief of all such factors. Such a cycle was stated to be the inevitable and intolerable result of a dependence upon competition to control the utilization of credit. Largely on account of the cycle's disastrous contributions to economic instability, there has been developed in the United States, in the Federal Reserve system, credit machinery designed to combat and to prevent the untoward consequences of the uncontrolled business cycle.[1]

When the Federal Reserve system was established it afforded adequate basis for a tremendous expansion of bank credit. This credit foundation was utilized to a considerable degree during the late war but not nearly to the limit of its capacity even then. Predictions were not lacking that this greater potentiality of credit expansion would be utilized forthwith. Those predictions, presumably, were based upon the assumption that competition would continue to control credit utilization. However, such has not proved to be the fact. Credit has not been expanded to the limits of the new banking system.

Undoubtedly some of the political leaders who were instrumental in the establishment of the Federal Reserve system, still clung to faith in the above-mentioned idol of

[1] Other factors contributed to the reorganization but they were subordinate. Most of them, like the difficulty of seasonal variation in credit demands were more or less closely tied up with the competitive administration of the old credit system.

the tribe.[2] The Wilsonian program in 1912 envisaged a reestablishment of effective competitive control. But, nevertheless, the machinery for credit control set up in the Federal Reserve system has not perpetuated competitive control in the banking field. The Federal Reserve Board has not depended upon competition to set limits to credit expansion.

The Federal Reserve banks are not competitive, money-making institutions. The truth is that so long as members of the Federal Reserve Board have regard for the practical consequences of their policies, they can not subordinate their actions to a régime of competitive control. If they were to keep the channels of credit expansion open and were to encourage it to expand to the limits of the system, the machinery which they control would only serve to multiply the ills which it is expected to relieve.

When the control of credit was in the hands of a competitively administered banking system, our economic machine ran amuck from time to time with persistent regularity. When reform was being discussed, there were many who advocated limiting changes to improvements of mechanism without disturbing the principle of competitive control. Had this policy prevailed the result doubtless would have made the periodic rampages of our economic system more severe than ever. Though perhaps not quite so frequent. As the situation is, the non-profit making, non-competitive administration of our

[2] *Cf.* the statement of Senator Carter Glass given to the press Sept. 9, 1927.

credit system cannot be expected to eliminate financial reactions altogether, but it can be and is expected to render conditions less intolerable than they were before. To do this the Federal Reserve Board must exercise the power which has been placed in its hands, and, in some fashion, drive the credit machine. So, whether the members of the Federal Reserve Board wish it or not, they are compelled to usurp the prerogatives of the tribal god.[3]

The significance of the foregoing commonplace analysis lies in the fact that it presents economic affairs in our own national unit as having passed out of the régime of competitive control. Whatever the degree of authority which competitive control still may have in more limited jurisdictions, its authority has been definitely superseded in the general sphere of control over our credit system as a whole. Nor is this change peculiar to the United States. In fact it came earlier in England than it did in the United States. However, the dominant financial position occupied by the United States since the late war has given world-wide significance to the development of such a régime in this country.

SOME MONETARY CONSIDERATIONS

There are those who see in the financial difficulties of various nations since the late war only a retribution fol-

[3] The depression of 1930-31 does not in any way invalidate the foregoing argument. The task of managing a credit system is not a lesson which can be learned over-night. However halting the administration of the Federal Reserve system has been thus far, the logic of the situation points to a gradual development of more and more constructive policies.

SOME MONETARY CONSIDERATIONS

lowing upon war-time inflation. Our own inflation in the United States is described as a more sophisticated form of the phenomenon but still essentially comparable to the greenback inflation of the Civil War period. That inflation is itself characterized as a more refined repetition of coinage debasement resorted to upon numerous occasions by European princes prior to the use of paper money.

If we are inclined to stress the fact of a recurrence of inflation and to abstract from its increasing sophistication as to form, we may observe that it typically accompanies war-time finance and may conclude therefore that it is a necessary and inevitable accompaniment of war. If, however, we are interested in the evolution of institutions, the observed recurrence of inflation is of minor consequence compared with the increasing sophistication of its form. When due consideration is given to the changing form of inflation, its continued recurrence no longer appears assured. Indeed it appears altogether unlikely. It is a long jump from coinage debasement to the credit expansion in the United States incident to the late war. The fact that, with a change of circumstance, the phenomenon has reappeared in different forms is no guarantee that it will continue so to reappear.

Credit, as an instrument of economic control, has grown up within a régime of competitive control. In its origin it was tied to the prevailing, competitively determined monetary or price unit. The contractual agreements of those who dealt in credit so placed it. But credit, as an important factor in the economic situation, has stayed hitched only in the sense that it has dragged the hitching post all over the lot. The money unit has been so dragged about at the heels of credit as to endanger its usefulness as a tool of economic organization. At least it was in the way of losing its effectiveness. Now, however, through a non-competitive control of credit, the money unit is being controlled as a matter of policy, that is, through machinery for the control of credit. As a result the money unit enjoys promise of rehabilitation as an acceptable measure of economic goods. But in the process of rehabilitation it has ceased to be either the product or the instrument of a régime of competitive control.[4]

In a managed currency, to use the current phrase for a credit system which is not competitively regulated, there is no inherent necessity for a gold or metallic monetary base.[5] The post-war efforts of various European nations to get back upon a pre-war gold basis rest, in part at least, upon inherited notions of a "natural," competitively determined "measure of value."

Competitive society, with its essentially subjective basis of organization, could not be expected to produce

[4] *Cf.* the address of the Right Hon. Reginald McKenna delivered Jan. 24, 1928, before a meeting of shareholders in the Midland Bank, Ltd. Mr. McKenna presented a summary review of the administration of the U. S. Federal Reserve system and discussed its relation to the world price level. In the course of this discussion he said,

"It follows, therefore, that it is not the value of gold in America which determines the value of the dollar, but the value of the dollar which determines the value of gold."

The address is reprinted in full in the *Acceptance Bulletin* for Feb. 29, 1928.

[5] Keynes, *Monetary Reform*, Ch. IV.

a stable money unit. This was not the fault of statesmen or economists of the period. It was inherent in the competitive organization. This organization, or system, was not consciously devised and imposed by a political authority. Its development through institutional reorganization was shaped by a more general cultural situation. And the influences which shaped the system as a whole at the same time determined its constituent features. Hence the development of a competitively controlled monetary measure of goods and services. And like the market itself, the money unit afforded only approximately accurate results. In the changed situation which has made necessary more accurate economic and social measurements, the passing of market control and the passing of the competitively determined money unit are as inseparable as were their origins.[6]

The above-mentioned efforts of European nations to get back upon a pre-war monetary basis are striking testimonials to the influence of the aforesaid idol of the tribe.[7] Those efforts are in reality evidence also of the support

---

[6] Of course the definition of the unit has always been a matter of legal determination. But whenever unlimited coinage of the standard money has been adopted, it has meant competitive determination of the legal unit's purchasing power. Such a situation prevailed until the appearance of controlled, non-competitive credit systems.

[7] This evidence of strength is not at all inconsistent with the general trend of the present discussion. It is quite possible for institutions, like individuals, to have great strength and fundamental weakness at the same time.

It might be said that a reluctance to trust administration of a managed currency to political authorities was responsible for efforts

which would be accorded a truly dependable common denominator for the exchange of economic goods.

We have in fact many yardsticks for effecting adjustment of economic claims. They include the ton, the gallon and the foot as well as the dollar. Economic goods must be described in terms of other yardsticks referring to their amount and quality before the money unit is applied to them. The striking fact in the history of the monetary yardstick has not been a greater popular readiness to change that particular measure. Rather it has been a persistent failure to recognize that the monetary yardstick has habitually changed. What would be necessary to place the customary money unit in a class with measures of length and weight in effecting economic adjustments is not a changed attitude towards the unit used but only the possession of one which compared favorably with the foot and the ton in stability.

Men would not now countenance a state policy by which the government would define a ton of goods bought by it as 2,500 pounds and a ton of goods sold by it as 1,500 pounds. Measures of the weight and bulk of goods have come to be so fixed a part of economic organization that their inviolability is taken as a matter of course even in war time. In the past, a régime of competitive control has imposed a money unit which did not share the stability of these other yardsticks. The relationships to which the money unit has been applied

of European nations to get back on a pre-war monetary basis. But this statement is only a negative expression of faith in the old policy of competition or laissez faire.

SOME MONETARY CONSIDERATIONS

have been conceived in consistently subjective terms. But now that a changed situation is bringing about a cultural reorganization upon the basis of an objective point of view, social organization will run in terms which can be expressed more objectively. That is, economic organization will tend to run in terms of volume of credit, output, discount rates, price levels and the like instead of in terms of utility, pain cost and individual choice. As emphasis is placed upon group organization, the individual must inevitably sink into the background.

A stable money unit may be counted upon to constitute one of the features of economic reorganization. In fact much of the development of such a unit already has taken place in the contemporary movement towards credit control. Present indications tend to support even the prediction [8] of John Stuart Mill with respect to an international monetary unit. Such an eventuality, it is true, is not in near prospect. The difficulties in its way are immeasurably greater than those which Mill foresaw. But current developments in the field of credit control; the study of relationships between monetary systems, and international cooperation to control exchanges tend to support the conclusion here based upon a general cultural change.

Soldiers and statesmen commonly insist that war will continue to be a recurrent feature of our culture. Grant-

[8] Mill was thinking merely of the use by all nations of one competitively determined, fluctuating unit. That is, the use of the pound or the franc or some other unit by all. The more significant development suggested here is a common stability even with the use of different units by different countries.

ing, for the sake of argument, that it does remain a part of our institutional heritage, the conclusion does not follow that the currency of a new régime will go the way of competitive monetary units of the past. The present movement towards stability of price levels is a movement away from competitive control. It is in keeping with the prevailing cultural trend. The development of a stable unit in a social structure founded upon the objective viewpoint may well result in a price measure which will successfully withstand the strains of even war-time finance.

CHANGE OF CONTROL NOT YET ACCOMPLISHED

It has long been a trusted argument in support of the theory of competitive control that the modern economic organization is much too complex and intricate a mechanism to permit of any control other than that of competitive regulation. This argument is losing its effectiveness. In a limited sense, our economic system already has passed from competitive regulation to the control of machinery which is not competitive. This, however, does not mean that a fully developed system of control has taken the place of the competitive market. The development which has taken place is merely a crossing of the Rubicon. The positive development of a new comprehensive system of control must come very gradually. But if the economist is to keep up with the march of economic development, he must, like Cæsar, turn his face forward to the coming campaign.

CONTROL OF SPECIFIC ECONOMIC PROCESSES

When we turn to specific economic activities we have a fruitful source of evidence with respect to current market control. Take at random, for example, farming, transportation, coal mining, meat packing, manufacture of automobiles, production and refining of oil, steel production, manufacture of electrical equipment, professional services, manufacture of agricultural equipment, production of lumber and building materials, banking, retail selling and labor. Frankly, there is a great deal of competition in all of them. More in some than others. But is this competition becoming more or less characteristic? Is there more of it than must inevitably hang over from a competitive period into an interregnum?

When we consider economic control with specific reference to such activities as those listed above, we immediately encounter farm bureaus, government commissions, trade unions, manufacturers' associations, trade agreements, trusts, retail merchants' associations with innumerable subdivisions, great corporations which spread out over many industries, gentlemen's agreements, professional ethics, tobacco growers' associations and literally hundreds of other similar agencies of economic control. These agencies have overrun the competitive system like a virulent growth of noxious vegetation. Their effect in some places has been to throttle competition entirely. In other places, however, they have merely set limits to it and thereby frequently have made it keener and more effective than before.

What, we well may ask, is the general significance of these agencies in relation to market control? They are practical arrangements hit upon to meet the needs of a current situation. They are concerned with immediate, active economic interests. They readily adjust themselves to a changing environment. They especially represent interests which are foreign to individualistic competition. They are not in any way concerned with the maintenance of a social ideal of any kind. They are not grounded in the fundamental law of the land but are, in the main, extra-legal. On account of their lack of either a traditional or legal rigidity they quickly reflect the influence of new situations. They provide a combination of social control and social fluidity. Because of this fact they are of very great importance in a readjustment of economic institutions. Although they are themselves exceedingly plastic, the influences which are working through them are slowly but surely reshaping an entire economic system.[9]

[9] "The growth of these cooperative organizations of independent business units represents, as I view it, a modification of the established organization of industrial control. Trade associations are progressively remodelling the system by which the productive and distributive processes are governed. By this I mean that the determination of the sorts of things produced, how they are produced, the volume in which they are produced and the conditions under which they are sold, is becoming more and more of a collective responsibility and a conscious decision. And it is, of course, becoming correspondingly less and less the chance outcome of the independent volition of numerous competing producers, as it has traditionally been supposed to be." M. W. Watkins, *American Economic Review*, Vol. 16, No. 1, *Supplement*, p. 231.

CONTROL OF ECONOMIC PROCESSES

The process of cultural readjustment may be likened to the moving-picture process of fading out one picture while a new one is taking its place. The two processes merge into one another. Disintegration of an old order leads to disorganization and the outcropping of a multitude of conflicting authorities. An immense mass of unofficial machinery of control develops. Disorganization leads to over-organization. This view of the process of institutional development throws light upon the over-organization which is now a characteristic feature of so many lines of activity. It is a symptom of the underlying cultural situation. The current period is one which demands a large and heterogeneous mass of institutional organization.

The appearance of a new cultural scheme necessarily involves a process of selection and organization. The integration of a new order must come about by the shaping of a system from materials present in a disorganized transition period. It is this process of integration which requires the guidance of a fundamental philosophical viewpoint. The formulation of a new system of law, the reconstruction of economic and political institutions and the making over of other forms of social organization must all be so coordinated as to afford a consistent, unified system for the adjustment of conflicting human interests.

The development of a new system of economic control is an integral part of a larger process of social readjustment. It is conditioned both by detailed developments in particular economic activities, such as those above mentioned, and by more general developments in non-economic activities. At the present time the appearance of a managed system of credit is highly important. But relative to the whole process, of which it is a part, it is a small matter. The members of the Federal Reserve Board could not by virtue of their position introduce a new régime of economic control of their own devising and volition. Their functions must be performed within fairly narrow limits determined by a great many different factors. The greater the insight with which their administration is conducted, the narrower will become the latitude of their discretion. In such a period as this the administration of such an instrument is like the current administration of law. It must be made an efficient mechanism. The evolution of financial institutions is only part of the economic aspect of social development. Making the Federal Reserve system an efficient mechanism involves its correlation with the details of economic activities, on the one hand, and with the broader developments of a cultural trend on the other hand. It is a matter of social engineering.

The problems of social engineering are not in their fundamental character different from engineering problems which deal with physical phenomena. They have been fundamentally different in the past only because we have thought about them in different terms. Our social philosophy has been different from our engineering philosophy. The administration of practical affairs is coming now to require the sort of insight which is afforded by the scientific point of view. This fact is both the cause and the justification of the current vogue of scien-

CONTROL OF ECONOMIC PROCESSES

tific education. Effective social engineering of the future must rest upon that sort of education.

It must be admitted that predicting the course of economic evolution is at present a hazardous and unsatisfying undertaking. It is no better than predicting the movements of the stock-market. When the market is low it is easy to predict that sooner or later there will be a sustained upward movement. At least under conditions as they have prevailed in the recent past such a conclusion has been so patent that it hardly merited the name of prediction. But it is quite a different matter to tell which upward movement is the beginning of a sustained rise.

So it is with respect to economic development. We know that a process of evolution is going on. We can even point out some of the larger outlines of the process. But when it comes to giving names and dates, so to speak, we are no better off than when we attempt to forecast the detailed movements of the stock-market. But we have come to a point which demands that we take an evolutionary point of view. And if we do take an evolutionary point of view we must do the best we can with attempts to chart the course of economic development. When the defenders of an individualistic system of theory tell us that we cannot understand the "inscrutable" ways of social evolution, it is as if they would say to the business man, "You must return to the 'hunches' of your predecessors, for you cannot, upon objective grounds, forecast economic developments."

When they say, "The movements of history are to be 'sensed' rather than plotted and projected into the future,"[10] their argument is wholly reactionary. It is an appeal from the scientist to the medicine man.

GENERAL SUMMARY

The cultural period which, in its economic aspect, was dominated by market control was characterized by the prevalence of an individualistic, subjective philosophy. But with changing circumstances, that point of view has lost ground to a more matter-of-fact, impersonal, objective viewpoint. How far this supplanting, scientific point of view is a result of machine technology and how far it is a cause of that technology is a question avoided in this discussion as not necessary or pertinent to it. The two are considered as different aspects of one process.

Disintegration of a common cultural philosophy must of necessity bring about a period of social conflict and disorganization. Such is the present condition of our culture. A demoralized cultural situation so brought about gives rise to the necessity for a maximum number of unofficial, temporizing agencies of control which enjoy only limited recognition. These agencies constitute a heterogeneous mass of machinery of control supplementary to the scheme of institutions holding over from a previous period. They represent a multitude of claims which conflict and coincide with each other in exceedingly complex patterns. These claims run sometimes in

[10] Frank Knight, "The Limitations of Scientific Method in Economics," in *The Trend of Economics,* p. 264.

terms of inherited rights but to a constantly increasing degree are in conflict with them. Out of this comparative chaos, unity and organization can come only through a process of selection from the mass of *de facto* machinery of control; only through the compromise and adjustment of conflicting interests in the formulation of a new system of law; only through a reconstruction of economic, political and other forms of institutional organization which will rest them squarely upon a single fundamental foundation. This means the introduction of a new philosophical basis under the prevailing institutional superstructure of society and a moulding of that superstructure to harmonize it with the new base.

In the present situation, the objective, or scientific point of view appears to be the only common meeting ground of widely divergent groups among Western peoples. The spread of this viewpoint is the most powerful influence in our current culture and is its most characteristic feature. No other philosophical viewpoint makes even a reasonable showing against it as a possible basis for cultural readjustment.

However, notwithstanding the fact that a cultural readjustment must rest upon a philosophical basis, it cannot be the work of professional philosophers or scientists. It must come about through a process of give and take on the part of all parties at interest in the adjustment. The special function of the social scientist, in the premises, is to formulate explanations or interpretations of social phenomena in objective terms like those of other sciences. Social reorganization upon the basis of an objective viewpoint means that men's actions with reference to social relations will come to be controlled by their knowledge of principles interpreting social phenomena just as their actions with reference to physical environments have come to be controlled by their knowledge of principles interpreting physical phenomena.

In the present situation, the decadence of an individualistic, competitive market control is evident. Changing conditions are altering even the point of view from which the immediate management of economic enterprise is conducted. It is becoming more and more objective and impersonal.

Accounting, the chief tool of management, likewise is undergoing a process of evolution. Accounting technique began as double entry bookkeeping. Accounting theory grew out of the application of double entry technique to actual business affairs. The changing needs of a changing economic situation have brought into accounting technique much statistical procedure not to be included in the double entry record. While accounts have increased in importance as an instrument of economic control, the supplementary technique not included in the double entry record has rapidly increased. Indeed the double entry record has become submerged in a much more comprehensive statistical record which is organized from a functional point of view.

Accounting theory likewise has undergone a process of development. Starting as a theoretical summary of the use of double entry records, it has become, or is rapidly becoming, a theoretical summary of the application of statistical methods to problems of public and private economic administration. Starting in a position entirely subordinate to the law of the competitive régime, accounting has become more and more independent in its viewpoint until it now commonly is depended upon by legal and administrative authorities for guidance in many decisions affecting economic interests.

As market machinery has become less and less effective in a changing economic situation, accounting technique has been developed to supplement and supplant it. So pervasive is this increasing dependence upon accounts that it suggests an organization of economic institutions around accounts comparable to the earlier organization around the market. Such a course of development is not suggested merely by the increasing importance of accounts in public and private economic affairs. It is corroborated by developments outside the field of economic control. Accounts are themselves becoming a subordinate branch of statistical technique. Statistical technique, in turn, is the chief agency through which the scientific point of view is making a conquest of social phenomena. The statistical method is both an instrument through which principles of social science are developed and an instrument through which those principles react upon and control the phenomena which they interpret. That is, they control such phenomena as well as interpret them to the extent that they control the actions of men which constitute social phenomena. Hence the prospect of economic organization around accounts is the economic aspect of a prospective cultural reorganization upon the basis of an objective philosophical viewpoint. Current developments in the economic field are thus of one pattern with developments in the broader process of cultural evolution.

While the competitive market has become less and less effective as an instrument of economic adjustment, competitive or market theory has thereby been rendered less and less applicable to current economic affairs. The methods of reasoning applied in the formulation of market theory have been such as to cause an entire disregard of this increasing rift between "theory" and fact. The result is that the theory of a competitive market has been applied to contemporary economic phenomena by means of a continually increasing *tour de force* in the shape of allowances for practical complications. It is therefore to be expected that the theory of the competitive market must sooner or later give way to some system which is drawn from current economic relationships instead of being merely applied to them by a *tour de force*.

The prospect of an economic organization around accounts suggests that accounting theory should be expected to take the place of market theory. But institutions and systems of theory do not come into existence full grown. Accounting theory is not now a general theory of economic organization. Hence the suggestion here referred to can only be that accounts and accounting theory promise to serve respectively as points of origin and organization for a reshaping of economic institutions and the development of a system of theory running consistently or primarily in objective terms.

It is a patent fact that important economic groups do not now have faith in market control. Indeed those who belong in one or another group of the faithless constitute a large majority of the population. They look to other agencies for protection of their economic interests rather than to their own efforts in a competitive market. Their trust is placed in a great variety of agencies. The resulting pluralistic condition of affairs is not what the physicists call a condition of stable equilibrium. The situation contains elements of danger threatening the continuance of our culture but the presence of a fundamental philosophical point of view to which a large majority gives allegiance and the economic advantage of a highly developed technique appear to afford ample basis for the prediction of a successful social readjustment.

In the meantime, Western civilization is undergoing a period of disorganization. At such a time the law breaks away from its earlier philosophical foundations. Although the law typically is called upon to serve the double duty of preserving a social ideal and effecting practical adjustments of conflicts, in a period of disorganization like the present the efforts of makers and administrators of law come to be devoted almost exclusively to the problems of practical adjustment. Of course a great deal of cheap political oratory harks back to an older social ideal but it may well be disregarded as inconsequential. However, with a new social adjustment, law will acquire a new philosophical foundation and the administration of law will again involve an emphasis upon the preservation of a social ideal.

Development of machine processes in the last 150 years has brought into the cultural situation a condition favorable to the spread of objective habits of thought. This influence has been especially potent in the sphere of economic organization. At the same time organization from an older viewpoint has been most firmly intrenched. In the conflict between the two viewpoints, the newer one has made headway rapidly in economic organization for production—in industrial and technological organization. But in the field of organization for distribution—in business enterprise and administrative control—the older viewpoint has held on more stubbornly. The result has been an economic system organized in part upon one basis and in part upon a different and contradictory basis. Only very gradually is the older basis giving way to the new in the development of a unified organization. But it *is* giving way. Administration, or business control, is coming to rest upon the same fundamental basis as technological organization.

In a transition period like the present, disorganization breeds over-organization. And out of over-organization must come reorganization. Analogies between social organization and biological organisms are only analogies but they are sometimes illuminating. The break in cultural organization is roughly analogous to a break in living tissues. A wounded organism throws reserves into the breech. Even in a clean wound there will result a surplusage of scar tissue which later is in part absorbed. So in the case of a breakdown in cultural organization, reserves of many sorts are thrown into the breach. Hence over-organization. Out of these reserves must be assembled the elements of a new organization. And in the process of integration of a new régime the institutional surplusage will disappear. It is this process of selection and integration which must be controlled by a philosophical viewpoint which thereupon becomes the foundation of a reorganized culture.[11]

Under the competitive régime, the responsibility falling upon the market was twofold. The market served to regulate specific economic activities and at the same time it was depended upon to afford an efficient operation of the economic system as a whole. An increasing failure of the market in both respects has been met on the one hand by the development of various unofficial agencies to regulate particular economic activities and on the other hand by the creation of a non-competitive

[11] It is not contended in this discussion that philosophical viewpoints shape the course of cultural evolution. Such a formula for interpretation of cultural development would only raise the question as to how the evolution of philosophical viewpoints is guided. Any method which singles out a given factor and holds that it dominates cultural evolution is dubious. The position taken in this discussion relative to the rôle of philosophical viewpoints is that cultural coordination or cultural unity is dependent upon the presence of a common viewpoint. Hence such a viewpoint may be a useful mark of identification and may even be a basis for forecast with respect to the emergence of a particular cultural scheme. This is not to say, however, that it is the only basis for such forecasting.

control of credit to provide a stability of the current economic system as a whole which the competitive market had failed to provide.

In the early history of the competitive system, before it became an established system in fact, its development was opposed by forms of social organization then prevailing. During that period there was an evident tendency for competition to prevail in spite of opposition. Fuller development of the individualistic cultural period brought this conflict to an end. In the more recent past a reverse conflict has set in. Competition has tended to languish in spite of laws designed to enforce it. These statements, of course, are generalizations subject to incidental exceptions, although in the main true. For reasons heretofore suggested, the prospect for the immediate future is not a continuance of the *status quo*. Neither is it a return to either of the two prior situations just mentioned. When we cease to attempt to enforce by legal enactment a general system of competition, we are not compelled thereby to prohibit competition. There are potent reasons why we should expect development of economic machinery of control to which a general support and approval will be accorded. There are also potent reasons why we should expect that machinery to afford a mutual checking and restraint of conflicting economic interests. And there are even more convincing reasons why we should not expect the market to provide the means of such mutual checking and restraint. At the same time, however, there is no reason to suppose that the market may not remain as a subordinate feature of economic organization. It is quite possible, indeed it seems highly probable, that an economic régime will develop upon the basis of principles which do not include either a prescription or a prohibition of competition. Economic control by the market will merely not be the fundamental feature of the system.

CHAPTER XVI
POSTSCRIPT

Whatever prediction is included in the foregoing chapters has been based upon the proposition that among occidental peoples an increasingly dominant objective viewpoint is becoming the foundation of a distinct cultural organization. It has been the intention of the writer to limit discussion strictly to such topics as bear upon the putative rôle of accounts in such an assumed development.

The purpose with which the foregoing discussion was undertaken was to relate accounts to other economic and social institutions, that is, to give them a social orientation. Since accounts are themselves obviously in process of evolution, any attempt to relate them to a static social analysis was out of the question. In the absence of a satisfactory theory of social development, the assumption of a cultural readjustment upon the basis of an objective viewpoint was hit upon as the most reasonable and useful hypothesis. It serves to interpret and correlate social developments not otherwise related. Incidentally, it makes possible the relation of accounting evolution to the broader process of cultural development.

However, this discussion has not been concerned primarily with argument in support of its fundamental hypothesis. Whatever argument has been advanced along that line has been only incidental. The intention has been to present a hypothetical analysis rather than to defend it. The hypothesis is not to be taken as a proved principle. But neither is it to be dismissed with a mere categorical denial. Before it can be disregarded, evidence against it must at least outweigh circumstantial evidence cited in its favor. Some other hypothesis must be found to better interpret the phenomena upon which it appears to throw light.

The writer feels very strongly that economic discussion, along with other studies of social phenomena, should be conducted with a most rigid fundamental adherence to the objective point of view. It seems to him a confusion of terms to apply the label scientific to any other sort of discussion. (Such a label is, however, of no particular consequence aside from its correct usage as a descriptive term. It has no ulterior efficacy.) This contention does not mean that the objective viewpoint is all comprehensive or self-supporting. It is not superior to but rather falls within the process of cultural development. In fact the writer's confession of feelings with reference to the use of an objective point of view indicates that, for him at least, the scientific movement is a cult with a non-rational foundation.

A colleague of the writer is such a believer in the objective viewpoint that he is unwilling to admit the possibility of its ever being supplanted. Such a position is understandable. Surely it is a logical possibility that cultural development should go forward under the constant dominance of an objective viewpoint. However, it appears to the writer that such a view errs in making an ultimate of the objective viewpoint and so leads one into the same blind alley which satisfies the subjective idealist when he says: "The world is such stuff as ideas are made of."

History does not appear to point in the direction of a millennium of any sort. It is more in keeping with the history of human cultures that the current cultural bias should in time give way to some other philosophy. The open mind which typifies the scientific point of view, it seems to the writer, should not be closed even with respect to the future of that point of view.

Including its rise, heyday and decline, the cultural scheme characterized in its economic aspect by organization about the market has lasted several hundreds of years. The cultural organization which appears now to be emerging runs in terms tremendously larger than those of the individualistic régime. At the same time the new régime appears to rest upon a philosophical foundation which is, at least, no less stable than that of the earlier period. Furthermore, there are reasons why we should expect a shifting of emphasis away from the economic aspect of culture. Therefore, it appears not to be within the bounds of reasonable expectation that cultural developments, which are here held to be going forward, should work themselves out in any period short of several hundred years. But, with respect to cultural development, a few hundred years is not in the long run. A workable theory of cultural evolution doubtless would run in terms much further beyond the reach of terms used in this discussion than the concepts here used are removed from the static analysis of a competitive market.

THE OBJECTIVE VS. THE SUBJECTIVE

It is not the purpose here to reargue at length the long-standing controversies among students of economics as to the relative merits of the static and evolutionary viewpoints and as to the relative worthwhileness of objective and subjective assumptions. However, some general consideration of these questions appears to be desirable at this point in order to place the whole discussion of preceding chapters in a proper perspective.

No small part of the recent impetus given to discussion of these questions in the United States is to be credited to the late Prof. Thorstein Veblen. Professor Veblen's arguments on behalf of the objective and evolutionary viewpoints have their greatest influence as an appeal to the current popular prejudice in favor of common sense, matter-of-fact knowledge. He appeals to the contemporary bias which has made a fetish of the word science. His effective sarcasm holds up to ridicule the methods of so-called static economics. The propensity of economic theorists to think in terms of normals he ascribes to an attenuated survival of early animistic thinking.[1] By implication the use of objective and evolutionary concepts is set up as something much better than a survival of primitive, animistic thought.

His own propensity for contrasts between the social

[1] *Cf.* "Why Economics is not an Evolutionary Science" in *The Quarterly Journal of Economics,* July 1898.

sciences and physical sciences, and his confident prediction that economics must adopt the viewpoint of physical science, may perhaps have carried Professor Veblen further than he intended. They appear to imply an expectation on his part that an evolutionary viewpoint in economics would concern itself only with the objective point of view. His anxiety to apply the philosophy of physical sciences to social phenomena led him to ignore persistent differences between the social sciences and physical sciences. We may well agree with him in adopting a monistic philosophy which assumes that physical, biological and social phenomena are expressible in common terms—that there is a unity running through them all. We might even agree that methods applying the objective viewpoint are the best available tools, or for that matter the only available tools, for interpretation of this assumed unity of experience. Nevertheless we must insist that a social study like economics cannot resort permanently and exclusively to the use of an objective viewpoint.

It has always been true that experience enforces upon men the practice of thinking sometimes in objective terms and sometimes in subjective terms. It must continue to be true until neurological and other complex physiological functions of the human organism are reduced to terms of mechanical equivalence or until the stimuli which play upon them become different from what they now are.

It may well be that the primitive savage and the simple-minded barbarian thought after the manner of classical

OBJECTIVE VS. SUBJECTIVE

economists. It is not to be held against them, or against the classical economists, if they did. A recurrence of emphasis upon subjective thinking is not a sign of reversion. Men of our own culture may well look forward to a time when subjective thinking will play a more active rôle in their affairs than it does today. Since human conduct has not been accounted for in objective terms, the different spheres of activity envisaged by the different social sciences are customarily unified through some sort of appeal to the subjective viewpoint. The particular unity which runs through social phenomena frequently must be interpreted as a subjective unity.

The foregoing statement appears on its face to be a denial of the fundamental contention in this argument that the objective point of view is serving as a basis for cultural reorganization. If social organization must involve subjective terms, surely it is foolishness to talk about cultural reorganization upon the basis of an objective philosophy!

The admission here allowed may not be as serious as at first appears. It is quite consistent to assume a unity of experience which is subject to expression and interpretation in objective terms and at the same time to recognize a subordinate unity of social phenomena running in subjective terms. To admit that we are unable to reduce all experience to assumptions underlying the objective viewpoint, and even to admit that this inability necessitates our use of subjective assumptions in dealing with questions of human conduct, does not involve denial of the major assumption that human conduct is of a common character with physical and biological phenomena. It follows from the major assumption, however, that social ideals around which a unified subjective interpretation of human conduct is organized, are comprised within the process which is to be interpreted in objective terms. Thus, if this major assumption is accepted, it follows that realism must ever be the true father of idealism, and the objective viewpoint must take precedence over the subjective even though both are indispensable.

The criticism against idealistic reasoning which can be brought upon objective grounds is not a charge that it is bad *per se,* but rather the milder charge that it habitually has refused to make obeisance to the objective viewpoint. In the hands of both laymen and professional philosophers, subjective idealism regularly has ignored or denied outright the humble position here allotted to it, and has attached to itself in some form or other the dignity of a religious mysticism. The dominant social ideals of each cultural group have acquired a sacred character in the eyes of members of that group.

This charge affords no grounds for putting a ban upon idealistic reasoning. All that the objective viewpoint of the realist requires is that idealistic reasoning be reduced to its proper rank subordinate to the objective analysis which is here held to interpret a broader basis of unity.

THE PROCESS OF INSTITUTIONAL DEVELOPMENT

Whatever may be the character of cultural evolution in general, the current segment from the life history of our own culture resembles the advance of an army against resistance. An army on the offensive moves forward from one strategic position to another. Each strategic position is held without further advance while previous gains are consolidated. Lines of communication are reestablished and services of supply are reorganized to meet the requirements of the more advanced position.

In terms of this simile, we have left one strategic position and are moving on to another. The position we have left was a unified cultural scheme in which human conduct was organized around a consistent group of religious, political, economic and other social ideals. (To this cultural scheme the adjective individualistic has been applied as a convenient term to describe it as well as a single term can.)

In moving on to a new strategic position we are groping more or less blindly. We have no data as to the long run objectives of the campaign of which the present movement is a part. And, as for generalship, we do not even know whether there is a general headquarters directing the movement. Our intelligence department is so shamefully incompetent that we do not even know the precise character of our immediate objective. We know, of course, that our reaching a next objective is not a question of time or place but a question of developing an efficient social mechanism. And such a mechanism is to be achieved through the formulation of a new scheme of social ideals to take the place of those which have been abandoned. But we are not yet able to forecast these new ideals which now are being shaped for us by a process of social evolution.

The current prevalence of faith in the objective viewpoint serves at the same time to undermine old ideals and as the chief instrument through which new ideals are to be drawn from an increasing knowledge of social phenomena. Through its undermining of unreasoned convictions relative to old ideals, the objective viewpoint makes for tolerance, and only through the practice of a great deal of tolerance can a given cultural group peacefully reorganize its institutional scheme.

Typically, in the past, institutional developments have been accompanied by intolerance and strife. The present period appears to be in a measure an exception to this rule. In spite of conspicuous exceptions, which soon wear themselves out, the peoples of Western culture exhibit a remarkable degree of toleration. This habit of tolerance supports the prediction of an earlier chapter in this discussion that, among English-speaking peoples at least, the present cultural revolution will work itself out peacefully.

Because this particular period is one of cultural advance rather than consolidation, a greatly enhanced significance is attached to evolutionary and objective concepts and methods. We have noted in an earlier connection that the application of the objective viewpoint has come to have a paramount survival value for the individual business enterprise. It now appears that a more general application of the same viewpoint has a no less significant survival value for the cultural group as a whole.

This monopoly of emphasis now enjoyed by the objective and evolutionary viewpoints is not permanent. In the course of time a new economic ideal will emerge along with other new social ideals. The cultural period following the emergence of these new ideals will be one of consolidation and organization rather than a period of evolution. Survival value then will lie in more emphasis upon the subjective viewpoint and upon the so-called static form of analysis. Discussions of economic value running in subjective terms, as all discussions of value should properly run, will again become pertinent and worth while. They will constitute part of the process of cultural consolidation.

THE RÔLE OF IDEALS

The objective viewpoint serves as a basis of cultural cohesion during the shift from one cultural scheme to another. It may also carry over into the new cultural organization if only the revival of subjective forms of thought is so held in check that their subservience to the objective viewpoint is recognized. If in subscribing to new ideals and in using them as guides to conduct, men recognize that all such ideals have been drawn from experience and are only tentative and temporary bases of organization, then the predominance of the objective viewpoint will have been preserved. An intelligent and qualified loyalty to ideals is a necessary condition of group survival but an unquestioning loyalty to inherited ideals is a sure method of social suicide.

The realist is not a man without ideals but only one who recognizes that his ideals are transitory and ephemeral. The only world the realist knows anything about is the world which comes under his observation. Ideals play an important rôle in that world but it is a subordinate rôle.

AN OBJECTIVE SOCIAL PHILOSOPHY

Because the objective viewpoint has afforded such significant results in physical terms, its rôle as a social philosophy has been neglected. It has suffered from the charge that it has to do with things which are temporal as contrasted with eternal verities claimed for the subjective viewpoint. Fortunately, this invidious comparison is losing its force. Even in the field of religion, the increasing influence of the objective viewpoint is to be observed. The current protestant schism between modernists and fundamentalists is a religious revolt against the dominance of a subjective social philosophy. The modernist has turned away from the literal following of religious traditions. He accepts the scientist's interpretation of a mechanistic world and is content with the doctrine that a spiritual authority works his will through the mechanism which is interpreted by the scientist in objective terms. This view accepts the objective viewpoint as its fundamental social philosophy. It rejects the notion of direct supernatural interference in human affairs. In its search for truth it turns from authoritative religious tradition to a study of the world in which men live. Thus the objective viewpoint becomes a tool by which those modernists who adopt it seek to understand and follow the will of God.

The only difference between such a religious position and the viewpoint of mechanistic science is in the assumption of deity back of the mechanism. So far as social theory and social policy are concerned this difference is of no consequence. While one man accepts the wisdom of experience as the voice of God the other heeds it as the only authority he knows anything about and without making any ulterior assumption. Thus, even in religion, the innermost stronghold of subjective philosophy, the dominant philosophy of this age is establishing itself to an ever-increasing degree.

When we speak in this discussion of a cultural scheme based upon an objective philosophy we do not mean one in which there is to be no social organization in terms of idealistic and subjective reasoning. The predicted cultural scheme is rather one in which men, as the prevailing rule, will subordinate their consciously idealistic and subjective thinking to their faith in results obtained by an application of the objective viewpoint; without bothering themselves with the philosophical puzzle involved in the fact that their faith in the objective viewpoint is itself subjective.

WHY THE OBJECTIVE VIEWPOINT CANNOT BE FINAL

It has been argued in the course of the foregoing chapters that emphasis upon an objective point of view is an inevitable characteristic of a transition period between cultural schemes which have distinct bases of unity. It is through an objective survey of a current social disorganization that men hit upon new ideals or new principles which will serve as foundation for cultural reorganization. Such a reorganization took place in northwestern Europe in the development of a modern, individualistic competitive or democratic social organization. And it is here contended that another such reorganization now is under way in Western culture.

It is an obvious and commonplace fact that such a reorganization as is referred to here involves a forsaking of old ideals and a following after strange gods. Undoubtedly in the history of human society there have been many peoples who have flourished and have disappeared because they could not adopt the new ways necessary for their survival. They have been supplanted by younger groups which were more vigorous because they were not hampered by a strait-jacket of outgrown institutions. And when particular civilizations have succeeded in making themselves over, it commonly has been with an accompaniment of violence and revolution, by the coming forward of new groups to positions of dominance and control.

As a civilization comes to rest more largely upon an accumulation of knowledge running in objective and impersonal terms, it is inevitable that it should adapt itself more readily to new conditions confronting it. Thus we can set up a scale beginning with those social groups which have been unable to survive for lack of power of adaptation. Next would come groups which have survived through adaptation but with a maximum of conflict and violence. Further up the scale would come in order those groups which have increased their powers of adaptation in the proportion that they have acquired ability to appraise crises in their social organization in objective terms. Following out the logical implications of this scale, we are led to the conclusion that eventually violence and revolution will be eliminated from the process of social change. A social structure in which the objective viewpoint is the controlling factor might well be expected to afford means of continuous adaptation. Just as an increasing knowledge of economic phenomena bids fair to eliminate the business cycle, with its heavy social losses, so an increasing knowledge of social phenomena gives promise of eliminating the cultural cycle with its much greater periodic social loss. Instead of alternating periods of transition and coordination, in which emphasis shifts back and forth from objective to subjective ways of thinking, we shall have, sometime in the future, so the argument runs, a stabilized cultural organization in which there will be a continuous balance between the problem of efficient social organization and the problem of adaptation; between static organization and evolutionary change.

The foregoing statement presents a tentative ideal or goal of social development. All that would be necessary to make it a final goal would be to make an ultimate of the objective philosophical viewpoint. But that would be just as bad as making an ultimate of technology or economic institutions or some other particular factor of cultural organization. When the writer adopted the objective viewpoint as a fundamental premise of the foregoing discussion, it was not with any idea of its being a final expression of wisdom. Any system of philosophy or philosophical point of view, as the mechanist must hold, is only a summary expression of ways of thinking or of the reactions of human nervous systems to stimuli. Objective and subjective ways of thinking have not created the social situations in which they respectively have been especially prominent. Rather they have been created by such situations. And if as a result of the development of such philosophies, among other causes, a stable social organization displaces a relatively unstable one, it follows that the stimuli afforded by the new social situation will be different in essential respects from those which were afforded by the old situation. And when such new stimuli are in their turn summarized in philosophical terms, it is to be expected that such new philosophical systems likewise will be different from their predecessors.

The formulation of a general theory of cultural evolution, it may be granted readily, is quite beyond our present powers of social analysis. But the more we study particular branches of social science, and the more effectively we relate them to each other, the better position we shall be in to make an appraisal of the process of cultural development. An approach toward the goal of making each branch of scientific study a center of human experience cannot fail to promote coordination of all such branches of study. In undertaking to present accounts as a focal point of cultural organization the writer has hoped to contribute something towards such a composite result.

The foregoing discussion has not been offered as a finished or comprehensive theoretical analysis. In some connections where the writer's resources might have permitted elaboration and more finished argumentation, it has been avoided as undesirable. The result sought was a sketch in broad outlines of the existing cultural organization and current cultural trend drawn from one particular point of view. The wide range of subject matter to be covered in the achievement of this result precluded detailed argumentation much as the innumerable details of natural objects are necessarily excluded from an artist's landscape.

These statements appear to place the present treatise in the somewhat paradoxical position of being an essentially artistic or subjectively unified argument for the use of an objective viewpoint. Such a paradox is, perhaps, not of serious consequence. The writer harbors no prejudice as to any ultimate superiority of one philosophical point of view over another. He does not accept any one of them as final or absolute. The desirability, not to say necessity, of a present application of the objective viewpoint in explanation of social phenomena does not rest upon any such notion of an ultimate validity of objective philosophical assumptions. Rather, as here argued, it rests upon the circumstance that an objective philosophy is the fundamental unifying influence in current Western civilization. Current culture, or at least our prospective culture, is to be explained upon the basis of objective assumptions because they constitute the foundation upon which it rests. They afford the basis for a distinct cultural type and so must be the means of interpreting it and distinguishing it from other cultural schemes.

APPENDIX A

CULTURAL EVOLUTION

The foregoing chapters have been sketched against a background of cultural development. For the student who wishes to make that background his chief interest, the following brief list of references is suggested as a basis for beginning his study. However, a student should be reasonably well grounded in both history and philosophy before he undertakes such a task.

Barth, P., *Die Philosophie der Geschichte als Sociologie.* Leipsig, O. R. Reisland, 1897.
Beard, C. A. (Ed.), *Whither Mankind.* New York, 1928.
Ellwood, C. A., *Cultural Evolution: A Study of Social Origins and Development.* New York, 1927.
Hegel, G. W. F., *Philosophie der Weltgeschichte.* Berlin, Georg Lesson, 1920-23.
Hobson, J. A., *Evolution of Modern Capitalism.* New York, Chas. Scribner's Sons, 1884.
Marvin, F. S. (Ed.), *The Unity of Western Civilization.* New York, H. Milford, 1922, 2nd Ed.
Ogburn, W. F. and Goldenweiser, A. (Eds.), *The Social Sciences.* Boston, 1927.
Pareto, Vilfredo, *Traité de Sociologie Generale.* Paris, Payot & Cie, 1917.
Sombart, Werner, *Der Moderne Kapitalismus.* Leipzig, Duncker & Humblot, 1917. (Revised Ed. 1928.)
Spengler, Oswald, *The Decline of the West.* New York, 1926.
Wells, H. G., *The Outline of History.* New York, 1922.

One who reads the foregoing list of references is impressed with the magnitude of the task of depicting cultural development. Too often those who have attempted the task have been guided by the dictates of particular schemes of interpretation. Spengler, for example, emphasizes those aspects of our own culture which fit in with his scheme of a typical cultural life history. The necessities of his scheme have led him to speak of the modern period of Western civilization as centuries of glorious skepticism after which our culture must revert to mysticism and to barbarism. The present writer would characterize those same centuries as a period of rather confused thinking which has been in the main dualistic. A philosophy of science has developed in a vast isolated laboratory of speculative thinking which has been made possible by the fact that a spiritual or subjective philosophy has been the backbone of social organization. This relative isolation of the philosophy of science cannot now be preserved. Both in the field of learning, or in the realm of the thinking of educated men, and in the world of practical affairs, this philosophy has outgrown its subordinate position. On account of the limitations of his scheme, Spengler misses entirely the prospect of what he would perhaps call a spiritual regeneration of Western culture under the influence of an objective philosophy.

Ellwood is not bound by Spengler's notion of a cultural life history. His recognition of a rhythm or cycle in cultural development is somewhat nearer the view presented in the foregoing chapters. He is limited by distinct patterns of his own, however, and his discussion is tinged by an incurable bias towards a fundamental subjective and spiritual viewpoint. Pareto, in the closing chapters of his second volume, comes still nearer to the view of cultural change presented in this volume but his position also is that of a dualist.

The subjective and spiritual bias of Hegel is too well known to be commented upon here. Even Wells betrays a conviction that "Through the ages one increasing purpose runs, and the thoughts of men are widened with the process of the suns."

The writer has endeavored to approach the problem of surveying the development of our own particular culture in a wholly objective fashion without any notion or scheme of the development of culture in general. The result has been a conclusion that the manner of such development in our own culture has changed and will continue to change. But in the writer's view we shall make progress in understanding cultural development by working from particular periods rather than by undertaking to set up general patterns of cultural development.

The work of Sombart furnishes an example of how one who is working in a field much narrower than cultural evolution in general may set up a pattern of social organization which is misleading because his view is not broad enough. Sombart sets forth the conception of an economic system as involving, (1) a moving spirit, (2) a plan and (3) the administration of a technology. In the capitalistic system these are, respectively, a spirit of business enterprise, the competitive system and machine technology.

It will be obvious that Sombart's view of capitalism as an economic system does not agree with the discussion in the present volume. According to the view which has been presented here an economic system would be one which is an integral part of a larger cultural system. On this basis, business enterprise and the competitive form of economic organization are associated with a cultural scheme which accompanied handicraft technology rather than the machine process. Capitalism, therefore, becomes a transition form of economic organization in which a type of control is carried over from a former period to administer a new technology during the early part of its history. In this sense, the guild control of handicraft might well be interpreted as a parallel to capitalism, as Sombart does in fact interpret it. But neither of them is an economic system according to the standard set up in the foregoing discussion. They are merely tentative transition adjustments lacking a fundamental coordination with other aspects of contemporary social organization.

The writer does not intend to condemn the above-mentioned discussions upon the ground that they exhibit particular patterns or schemes of cultural development. One can accept such schematic interpretations as illuminating without acknowledging them as descriptions of cultural change. Nor does the writer delude himself with the idea that his discussion is free from the display of a particular pattern. He does, however, believe that it approaches more nearly a description of the change of our own culture than does any of the discussions here mentioned, in the sense that it adheres more closely to a fundamental assumption that social phenomena are explainable in objective terms. This assumption has prevented the drawing of a pattern in sharply defined lines. The result should therefore be more readily combined with other patterns resting upon the same fundamental assumption in a still nearer approach to a description of the process of current cultural change.

APPENDIX B
COMPETITIVE ECONOMIC THEORY

A thoroughly logical treatment would have required a chapter on the development of competitive economic theory to precede a discussion of its decadence, just as the chapter on "The Rise of Market Control" precedes the one on "The Disintegration of Market Control." With respect to the problem of value, such a chapter would point out how the comparatively naïve conception of Adam Smith was developed into the sophisticated pain cost concept of the classical school and how the latter was effectively buttressed by Ricardo's theory of rent. It would point out, as Veblen did, how the utility school merely shifted the emphasis of the discussion from production to consumption and from pain cost to utility without disturbing in any way the subjective philosophical foundations of the theory. Continuing the interpretation it would point out the establishment of an equilibrium of emphasis in the writings of more recent economists, as for example in the work of Alfred Marshall.

On the side of distribution such a discussion would point out how the naïve physiocratic conception of productivity was followed by the scarcely less naïve conception of Adam Smith, which in turn is carried on into Mill's distinction made between productive and non-productive consumption as well as productive and non-productive labor. It would show that, under the later influence of the utility school, productivity comes to be an exact parallel to the concept of utility. Thus there comes to its complete logical development, a unified system of competitive theory applying to both production and consumption: to both value and distribution.

This picture of the development of a system of competitive theory should be accompanied by an account of the work of the early German and English historical economists and that of their lineal descendants, the more modern institutional and statistical economists. A discussion of the historical, genetic, institutional and statistical viewpoints would bridge the gap between a description of the development of competitive economic theory and a discussion of its sterility and decay.

The writer was deterred from presenting such a discussion in the foregoing chapters both by the magnitude of the task and by the fact that, if it were done effectively, it would throw the discussion out of balance with respect to its primary purposes.

INDEX

Accounting,
  Control function of, 203
  Definition of, 217
  Development of, 209
  Problems, 200
  Profession, 239
  and institutional reconstruction, 234
  and management, 213, 221
  and the market, 197, 205
  and statistics, 208, 237
  theory vs. economic theory, 240, 258
Accounting Control,
  and market control, 258
  not yet established, 274

Business Management,
  A revolution in, 144
  Responsibilities of, 150
  Statistical methods in, 149
  and accounts, 213
  and the machine process, 144, 219
  and technology, 137, 141
Business Unit,
  Evolution of the, 138
  Increased survival power of the, 255

Cassel, Gustav, 87
Chapter Contents,
  Preliminary statement of, 4
"Commercial Revolution," 56
Cooperative Research, 16
Cultural Evolution, Appendix A
Cultural Philosophy
  Significance of, 30
  Objective vs. subjective, 300
  No finality in objective, 301
Cunningham, 27

Economic Control,
  Past and present, 265
  De facto, 275
  Cf. Market Control

Economic Interpretation of History, 26
Economic Theory,
  Competitive, Appendix B
  Definition of, 88
  Development of, 8, 85
  A new, 103, 232
  vs. accounting theory, 240
Ellwood, C. A., Appendix A
Eucken, Rudolph, 115

Federal Reserve System, 266
  Policy of the, 267
Friday, David, 93, 96, 99

General Summary, 280
Government,
  Accounting control and, 237
  The nature of, 226

Hegel, G. W. F., Appendix A

Ideals,
  The rôle of, 299
Individualism,
  Origins of, 39
  and handicraft industry, 44
Industrial Revolution, 53, 59, 137
Inflation, 269
Institutions,
  Accounts and reconstruction of, 234
  Development of, 296
  Kinship of, 15, 229

Laissez Faire, 34, 265
  Cf. Market Control
Law,
  The nature of, 177
  The philosophy of, 180
  Present outlook for, 189
  Merchant, 59
  and the market, 184
  and science, 130
Luther, Martin, 48

INDEX

MacDonald, J. Ramsay, 111, 114, 187
Machine Process,
  and science, 125, 133
  and management, 144, 219
Market,
  Declining significance of the, 35
  Limitations of the, 194
  and accounting, 194, 197, 205
  Cf. Market Control
Market Control,
  Agricultural distrust and, 71
  Establishment of, 59
  Factors affecting development of, 57
  Government regulation and, 76
  Labor's attitude towards, 73
  Prerequisites of, 38
  Theory of, 37
  and accounting control, 258
  and the business cycle, 78, 266
  and the industrial revolution, 53
  and large scale production, 67
Marx, Karl, 40, 111
Mitchell, Wesley C., 104, 249

Objective vs. subjective viewpoints, 22, 293

Pareto, Vilfredo, Appendix A
Perry, R. B., 97 and following
Pluralism in Political Theory, 64
Pound, Roscoe, 130, 183
Profits,
  Accounting view of, 255
  The rôle of, 252
"Pure Science," 24

Renaissance, 46
  in Italy, 52

Sabine, G. H., 65
Schools of Business, 154
Science,
  Future of, 132

Science (Cont.)
  Methods of, 120
  Philosophy of, 117
  Social phenomena and, 124
  Technology and, 125, 133
  and law, 130
Scientific Management, 162
Smith, Adam, 35, 249, 252
Socialism,
  Philosophy of, 111
  not revolutionary, 115
Social Readjustment,
  The process of, 157, 277, 296
  in economics, 230
Social Theory,
  Development of, 14
Sombart, Werner, Appendix A
Spengler, Oswald, 230, Appendix A
Standardization,
  Cultural, 161, 172
  and technology, 167
Statistical Method,
  in management, 149
  in science, 122
Statistics,
  Relations to accounts, 208, 211, 237

Taylor, Frederick W., 163
Technology,
  Future of, 169
  Standardization and, 167
  and business management, 137, 141
  and science, 125, 133
Toynbee, Arnold, 54

Value Theory,
  Appraisal of, 91
  Criticism of, 96
  Problem of, 93
Veblen, T. B., 125, 132, 293

Wells, H. G., Appendix A

Young, A. A., 11, 128, 258